THE
INSTANT
PRODUCTIVITY
TOOLKIT

21 Simple Ways to Get More Out of Your Job, Yourself and Your Life, IMMEDIATELY

LEN MERSON

Founder and CEO, Productivity Concepts, Inc.
Creator of the CareerTech© Program

SOURCEBOOKS, INC.®
NAPERVILLE, ILLINOIS

Published by Sourcebooks, Inc.
P.O. Box 4410, Naperville, Illinois 60567-4410
(630) 961-3900
FAX: (630) 961-2168
www.sourcebooks.com

Merson, Len.
    The instant productivity toolkit : 21 techniques for getting more out of your job,
yourself and your life, immediately
        p. cm.
    ISBN 1-4022-0330-6 (alk. paper)
    1. Paperwork (Office practice)--Management. 2. Time management. 3. Records--
Management. I. Title.

HF5547.15.M47 2005
51.5--dc22

                                                            2005012502

Printed and bound in the United States of America
BG   10 9 8 7 6 5 4 3 2 1

*H*ow many of us, growing up, ever got up in the middle of the night to go to the bathroom, and came back to find that our mother had made the bed? How many of us ever found that if we ever messed up the "junk drawer" in our mothers' kitchen, we got into trouble? I wish to thank my mom for planting the seeds which began my career so early in my life.

As early as the 1940s, my father had a small leather notebook in which he used to write pertinent information, as well as log expenses, phone numbers, etc. Unknowingly, he very well may have designed the first professional organizer. I wish to thank my dad for giving me the mental tools to begin my career.

Contents

Preface

In the early 1970s, I was conducting sales and marketing consulting with companies when I began to realize that, on a personal level, they were all so badly disorganized that it was getting in the way of my helping them. Without being asked, I took it upon myself to get them organized, focusing on how their employees handled their particular workloads. What transpired with each and every client was that sales began to shoot up like a rocket—and I hadn't even begun my sales and marketing support!

I began to see clearly the powerful correlation between organization and sales, organization and revenue, organization and profits. Yet the one that had me most surprised was the correlation between organization and the self-esteem of people within each of these organizations.

As I looked around our business community on a national scope, I noticed that there was no training company dedicating itself to the human side of information management. Not software, not hardware, not time management, not theory; rather, the real world of people interacting as proactive individuals with the massively growing amounts of information inundating them all at every given moment. My response was to change the nature of my business and start specializing in personal organization. By that I mean helping individuals take control of their workloads by more efficiently handling their information flow. My business grew rapidly, and today I can proudly say that my training programs have helped tens of thousands of people, both in the United States and abroad, take control of their workloads by "taking back their desks."

I am very much aware that organization just for the sake of being organized is futile. My training programs do not just help my clients keep their offices and cubicles tidy and attractive. They also give them priceless tools that enormously increase their personal productivity, keep them on top of their schedules, and allow them to go home at the end of a typical workday without having to worry about tasks undone.

And that's what organization is all about. Organization is a means, not an end. A means to take us to a joyous place of high personal productivity and peace of mind.

In my consulting business, I have a mission statement which ends with "to recapture your life." That is the major motivation of my consulting and training work—and my reason for writing this book. I help my clients recapture their lives by freeing up time they would otherwise be losing to the chaos of their disorganization. And I want to share the secrets of my method with you, my valued reader.

In other words, I want you to see *The Instant Productivity Toolkit* as a means to a greater end—reclaiming the proper balance between your work and your life.

How many people do you know who, at the end of their lives, have said, "I wish I'd spent more time in the office and less with my family"? How many say, "Gee, I wish I hadn't taken so many vacations" or "I wasted so many hours on my favorite hobby when I should have been working myself to a frazzle"? Probably not very many. Even in the middle of our lives, most of us who have regrets have them about the time we *don't* spend with friends or loved ones, or in activities that we truly relish and value. I hope this isn't you, but if you feel yourself thinking in these terms—even occasionally—it's time to correct the situation. This book will help you act positively to pursue your life's priorities.

Do you know what gives me the greatest satisfaction? It's when I meet up with people whom I've helped restore the balance between their work and their lives, and they tell me, "I'm back coaching my kid's Little League team." Or they say, "I don't stay glued to my desk until nine o'clock at night any more; I'm leaving at five or five-thirty, and I'm actually completing *more* work." Or, "I no longer find myself 'vegging out' in front of the TV in the evening; when I go home, I am actually a real human being. What a change!"

Those are testimonials from folks who have followed my plan and turned their lives around. Such stories as these are the greatest reward in my profession, and it will please me no end if you, too, turn your life around as a result of reading this book.

I want *you* to master your workload and restore your work/life balance as you want it. If this happens because you have read my book, then I have fully accomplished my goal.

Len Merson
San Diego, CA
February 2005

Acknowledgments

David W. Paul, my writer and editorial consultant. Without David's incredible perseverance, commitment, and inspiration, this book would have been an eternal figment of my imagination.

Wright Thomas ("W. T.") Arnold, my original collaborator. This remarkable young man's guidance and tenacity enabled me to launch this work. In so doing, "Dub" gave me a mere glimpse into the commitment of supreme athletes.

Stephanie Kip Rostan, my wonderful agent, who believed in, and constantly pushed for, both me and my project.

Jessica Marie "Guru" Larivee Merson Niles, my astounding daughter. Since very early childhood, "Gu" has taught me more about life, its joys, its blessings, and its lessons to be learned, than any other person I have ever encountered on this planet.

Shiva Beroukhim for her tireless administrative support and her ability to interpret my hieroglyphics during the embryonic stage of this work.

Michael Ward, for having the courage to be the best devil's advocate and greatest friend one could ever hope to have.

Allan Lewin, my brother, who has supported me over the years in ways that only a brother could.

Paul Niles, my wonderful son-in-law, who has been an inspiration as a husband to my daughter, father to my grandsons, and member of my family.

And also to the following, for their contribution has been greater than I believe they realize: Hillel Black, Allison Thomas, Todd Stocke, Michelle Schoob, Marty Kahn, Fred Raskin, Pamilla "Sam" Wessling, Lynne Allen, Dr. Bert Krasnoff, Sherman Lew, Barbara Spector, Larry Braun, Jim Tenuto, Mare Grace, and Natalie Ventula for her particular undying support.

INTRODUCTION

How Did My Life Get Out of Balance?

In twenty minutes, Jim is due to present the latest sales figures at a staff meeting. He worked hard to produce his report, but now it's lost amid the clutter of papers and folders on his desk. He searches through the slush piles on the floor and credenza behind him, and feels his blood pressure rising. Did he at least save the document in his computer? No way will he find it there; his computer files are chaotic.

Chaos in Jim's life is altogether too familiar. The files and folders, the inter-office memos, the email, the voice-mail—he's so far behind, he doesn't know if he'll ever catch up. It's a chronic condition, same as last week, last month, last winter. His family life is suffering from it. Jim's work keeps him from spending quality time with his wife Sarah and his two kids, Todd and Jill. They're not happy about it, and neither is Jim. Something has got to give.

Fast-forward one month: Jim is at a soccer game, sitting with Sarah and Jill. It's the first time he's gotten out of the office in time to see Todd play. He has caught up with his workload, and he is guilt-free. He's thinking about the change that has taken place—when suddenly, out on the field, Todd kicks his first goal ever! Jim thanks his lucky stars that he's there to see it happen.

Now picture Jenny. Jenny is in a different profession but a similar predicament. She has a great job, and when she took it, she thought she was on the road to achieving her life's goals. Her position involves a lot of responsibility and pays a comfortable salary. She was looking forward to a happy personal life, some exciting travel adventures, volunteer work for the symphony; and she thought maybe she'd start practicing on her own, long-neglected cello once again.

That was the dream. The reality is that she takes her briefcase home full every night and works most weekends. She's losing sleep, worrying that her upcoming holiday trip to see her family will put her even further behind. And forget about that snorkeling vacation off the Great Barrier Reef two months from now; Jenny is convinced that if she takes the time off she'll never catch up.

What has Jim learned that Jenny needs to know?

Jim has not uncovered the philosopher's stone or waved a magic wand. He has learned to apply twenty-one simple but priceless techniques that I have developed over many years' experience in helping people like him. The twenty-one techniques have empowered Jim to get his job under control and recapture spare time—something that had become foreign to him. Now his life and his work are in a much better balance.

You can do it, too. If there's anything in Jim's former situation or Jenny's current plight that sounds familiar to you, keep reading. You are about to experience the transformation that turned Jim's life around.

Two Days to Chaos

It only takes two days to enter the world of chaos. The first day, work comes flying at you from eighty-four different directions, and you are supposed to review, assimilate, process, and complete it all before tomorrow. At the end of this day, you've completed a decent percentage of the work. However, there is still a lot that you haven't done—even though you ate lunch at your desk and stayed in your office late. Now comes the second day, and you have all of the work that you didn't accomplish from yesterday *plus* all that will pile up today. *Voila*...you have officially entered the world of chaos.

The good news is that there is hope. There is a way to manage your work flow and conquer the chaos.

It's Not Your Fault

But wait, you may say, am I to blame for the mismanagement of my work?

No, absolutely not. I want you to understand that *no one* is to blame—least of all, you. So please discard that notion. Throw it out the window.

Instead of playing the blame game, let's focus on what to do. Chances are, you've never learned an effective methodology for managing your work. And unless you've attended one of my classes or been trained in my system, you've never been exposed to the single most effective approach to managing your work. This book will teach you how to easily put my approach into operation and how to use it so that you will never again fall behind in processing the information that makes up your workload.

> Discard the notion that you are to blame, and focus on what you are about to learn.

Countering the Advantages of Being Disorganized

Huh? The advantages of being *dis*organized? How can there be any advantages to disorganization?

I've worked in information management for more than thirty years, and I've heard every excuse imaginable for being disorganized. Some people actually believe it is better to be disorganized, and even to work amid clutter. Here are a few of their reasons:

- I've made myself an indispensable part of this company. If they ever fired me, they'd never find anything. Nobody would want to sort through my clutter to complete my tasks.

- I look busy. Nobody's going to give me more work, because they believe I'm drowning in the work I've got.
- The piles of paperwork on my desk tell people I'm important.
- My manager won't cut my salary, because it's obvious that I work hard.
- I know where everything is in those stacks. If I rearranged them, I wouldn't know where anything is.

It doesn't take a great insight to see through these arguments. They are all about image and illusion: the image the person wants to project to his or her manager and workmates, and the illusion that this person is working productively. In fact, what we're seeing are lack of order and the sure signs of low productivity.

> There is every good reason for being organized and having efficient work habits.

If you hear yourself making excuses for your mess, take warning. Tell yourself the truth: There is *no good reason* for being disorganized, no positive benefit to be derived from clutter, no advantage to sloppy working habits. There is *every reason* for being *organized*. There are unlimited benefits to cleaning up your clutter and developing efficient work habits.

What You Will Learn from This Book

In the chapters that follow, you will learn my tried-and-true techniques for managing your information flow, organizing your workspace, establishing a positive, healthy discipline, and *gaining control*

Frequently Asked Question
What are the "Black Holes" of information?

"Black Holes" are my term for places in your workspace where information gets lost. As you probably know, astronomers have identified black holes in outer space as extremely dense objects whose gravitational pull is so strong that anything in their field of gravitation gets sucked in, never to come out again.

There are certain areas in everyone's office that resemble black holes in that they suck in documents, memos, letters, and other important objects containing information as if devouring them. Unlike with true black holes, it is usually possible to retrieve the lost information, but it can be difficult and time-consuming. I call these treacherous regions the "Black Holes" of information. They include the following:

- Trays and standing file folders
- Paper files
- Multiple calendars
- Computer files
- Email In-box
- Voice-mailbox

Unless you treat the "Black Holes" of information with special care, information that enters them has a tendency to disappear and stay hidden when it is needed. We'll discuss how to deal with them in the course of this book.

for the rest of your life! You will learn how to set realistic goals that will give you time for the people and activities you truly value—family, recreation, hobbies, and your own personal quiet time—and you will set in motion a plan to achieve your goals.

Specifically, you will learn how to:

- Stay on top of your work, measurably increase productivity, make fewer mistakes, and be more creative in your work
- Have a clutter-free desktop and an attractive, inspiring office environment
- Eliminate the "Black Holes" of information in your office
- Have an empty email In-box at the end of every working day
- Enjoy the *pleasure to forget*—because you will have greatly diminished your stress

I am confident you will find that all of the twenty-one techniques described in this book are helpful. You may apply them as they make sense to you, as many as you are able to use. However, if you apply *all* of them, according to the directions I lay out in the section titled "For the Virtuoso" (see pages 169–204), I believe you will find my approach to be life-changing. My twenty-one techniques will take you beyond the tangible act of changing your filing systems and teach you a new paradigm of personal management. Just as athletes train to increase their efficiency of movement, you will train yourself in the skills and habits of personal productivity. When memos or documents land on your desk or in your computer, you will know how to handle them for prompt action or store them for instant retrieval. You will learn to minimize distractions and avoid costly errors.

Once you become a "virtuoso" at using my techniques, you will feel your stress level lower dramatically. You will find it easier to sleep, free from worries about whether you returned all of your urgent phone messages, whether you remembered to write down all of tomorrow's meetings and tasks, and whether you can instantly retrieve your important documents when you need them. You will get up in the morning and arrive at the office to find your desk clear and ready for a good day's work, and you will sail into the day knowing you have everything under control.

The pleasure to forget

When you have mastered the twenty-one techniques, you will experience the "pleasure to forget." This does not mean you will cheerfully miss meetings, show up late for appointments, or neglect assignments. Obviously, there are certain things you should never forget.

But there are definitely some things you should forget. You should have the pleasure to forget your anxiety about follow-ups. You should have the pleasure to forget what it's like to wake up in the middle of the night realizing you didn't get back to a client about a contract that had to be signed by the end of the day yesterday. You should have the pleasure to forget what it's like to be consistently late returning home for dinner. And you should have the pleasure to forget what it's like to be tired out, stressed out, and constantly out of sorts. Believe me, it is one of life's greatest pleasures to forget such things as these. Look forward to it.

A means to an end

Getting your work under control and getting more out of your work are only the first benefits I want you to get from this book. Reaching your maximum productivity and achieving greater creativity on the job are worthy objectives, but not the ultimate goal. I want you to think of these goals as a *means* to a *greater end:* reclaiming a balanced life. Your work is important, no question about it. But so is your personal life, your family life, your life of friendships, hobbies, "extracurricular" interests, vacation, and relaxation. You know it's important to bring your work into balance with the rest of your life. Here's your chance to do it.

And What About Jenny?

Remember Jenny, whom we met a few pages ago? The woman whose path to self-fulfillment and a balanced lifestyle got sidetracked by the chaos at work?

Don't worry about her. She recently had a heart-to-heart talk with Jim, and he told her about his discovery. Jenny has a copy of the book you are now reading, and she is learning how to apply my techniques to her job. She may even get to the Great Barrier Reef this year.

And now it's your turn. Your turn to learn the most efficient system for organizing your office space, a process for prioritizing your tasks, and a system for flowing your work through predictable stages in an unpredictable world. Your turn to experience the "pleasure to forget." Your turn to heave a sigh of relief, toast your success, and begin to dream and plan for how you will turn your spare time to activities you have long looked forward to. It's time to get more out of your job, yourself, and your life.

PART I

The Twenty-One Techniques

Imagine yourself feeling in control of your work. You are known around your organization for finishing all assignments on schedule. You are on top of your email, and you never have a backlog of unanswered phone messages. You never have to say, "Oh, no, I let that slip," or, "Where did I put that _____?" You vaguely remember those days when you heard yourself repeating, like a mantra, "I don't have time." But now you do.

Is it just a dream?

Many of us fall behind in our jobs and blame ourselves. We haven't learned how to control our time. We're not working hard enough. If only we'd paid better attention during that time-management workshop, if only we could be better organized, if only…

The fact is, our problems are not about time management. If you've attended a time-management seminar, you may have sat in a hotel ballroom surrounded by a couple hundred people and listened to a speaker who is witty and entertaining. All in the audience paid rapt attention and nodded their heads frequently in agreement, including you. After the euphoria of the lecture, however, your motivation probably began to wane. You got back to your office and saw your In-box overflowing. Within a day or two you were again buried in work, and all those notes you took were lying on a shelf somewhere.

There is a fundamental fallacy in the concept of time management. In fact, time cannot be managed. Time marches on, as the old cliché goes, and there is nothing you or I can do to stop it or control it. We cannot rearrange it. We cannot buy more of it. Although we are accustomed to talk about "killing time," in fact that is only a figure of speech. Can you imagine turning on the evening news and hearing the newscaster say, "A local resident was arrested today for killing time"?

It doesn't make sense, does it? What we can do is kill opportunities by not taking advantage of them. That's not good.

If we cannot manage time, we can manage ourselves: our working patterns, our environment, and *the way we use our time*. We can establish efficient habits, greatly minimize distractions, prioritize our tasks for the best results. We can always keep our working papers and computer files instantly retrievable. And instead of killing opportunities, we can grab up lost opportunities by having a foolproof system in place that allows for doing our work in far less time.

Do we have too much work? Our first inclination might be to say yes, we do, and there is evidence that would seem to support this. Our twenty-first century world shoots information at us at stress-inducing speeds. Fifteen years ago we were told the electronic age was leading us to the "paperless" office, but since that rosy scenario was first painted, paper consumption in the United States has tripled. In the same time, our computer systems have accumulated terabytes of electronic data. For many of us, the "information revolution" has become a nightmare of disorganization and information mismanagement. Paper overflows our desk trays; email and voice-mail compete for our attention. It is too much for us to handle—unless we change the way we approach our work.

It's not the *amount* of work that puts us in a state of chaos; it's the *mismanagement* of it. What we need is to learn a better way to manage our work, especially our information flow. We need to work smarter, in a more organized fashion. Not just *any* organized fashion, but in a way that makes us truly productive and truly creative. That's what these twenty-one techniques will help you to do.

The Essentials

In all worthwhile undertakings, there are certain steps you must take or else you will never achieve your goal. So, too, with my productivity-enhancing techniques. In this chapter, you will learn five techniques that form the basic steps along the road to changing the way you manage your work and your time. These techniques are like the hammer, the saw, the tape measure, the nails, and the level in a carpenter's toolkit: Nothing can get done without them.

It all starts with your physical environment

The first requisite for getting your work under control is making your office or cubicle an attractive and efficient environment. Being organized throughout your entire space is essential to working at your full productivity.

The second requisite is setting up the basic tools for processing your workflow. These tools are necessary if you are to develop the efficiency habits that will enable you to achieve your goal of maximum productivity.

Easier said than done, you're probably thinking, and you're quite right. Old working patterns can be hard to break. New habits do not come instinctively. But if you didn't want to make a positive change, you would not be reading this book. Trust me: I know what it takes to turn your life around, and I'm going to teach you how to do it.

TECHNIQUE #1:
The Purge
Make your physical space an efficient and attractive working environment

The first technique, the *purge*, is the place to start for rescuing your office or cubicle from the chaos of clutter and the mismanagement of your work. During the purge, you will revamp your workspace and reconstruct some of your information-management tools. You will give your physical space the look and feel of an environment made for efficiency and focus.

"Purge" may sound like a harsh word with extreme connotations. At certain times in history, the word has had a terrible association with cleaning out the ranks of a political elite. In religious terminology, the term means getting rid of sin or defilement. In the medical sense...well, let's not go there.

But fear not—none of these meanings pertains to what you are going to do. You will find the purge a *positive* process that will give you a feeling of accomplishment. You will lose the disorganization that is keeping you from moving forward, and you will gain a new way of putting order into your workspace. And if you pursue the entire program outlined in this book, including "Part II, For the Virtuoso," this could be *the last time for the rest of your life* that you will ever have to carry out the purge of your office.

The purge is the only complex technique in this book. The process entails six steps, plus some preliminary actions that I call "Step Zero," and depending on how much clutter there is in your office, it might take some time. I usually tell my clients to allow up to four to six hours, but you might be able to complete it faster if your workspace is only moderately cluttered or less.

Step Zero: Preparing for the Purge

"Step Zero" is not exactly a step. It is about making a commitment and putting in place a few supplies you will need for the purge.

Make an appointment with yourself

I strongly urge you to formalize your commitment to the purge by making an appointment with yourself. Enter the appointment in your calendar, book organizer, or personal digital assistant (PDA) and think of it as you would any appointment with another person. Keep the appointment. Do not let anything else take priority for the time you've scheduled.

How much time should you reserve for the purge? If your workspace is in pretty good shape, you might only need a morning for the purge. If it's a disaster area, it could take you eighteen hours. In my experience, most people underestimate the amount of time. My advice is to first read through the steps in this chapter so you know what you'll be doing; make your best estimate of the time you'll need, and then multiply that by 1.5. If you think it will take you four hours, reserve six hours. If you think it will take six, reserve nine.

Make an appointment with yourself to carry out the purge.

Weekends are an ideal time for the purge, for two reasons: first, it's easier to avoid distractions on the weekend; and second, you won't be eating up valuable weekday hours. It is possible to purge your workspace during the week, but it's not the best idea. Every normal office has its inevitable distractions—the telephone, email, inter-office mail, that meeting the boss says you have to attend. Your workmates will stick their noses in your door, curious about what you're doing, and they will want to chat. No matter how firmly you resolve to keep your mind on the task, you will probably succumb to some of those distractions. If you really must conduct the purge during the week, be tough about reserving enough time.

The most important thing, whether you carry out the purge on a weekend or in midweek, is that you *keep the appointment.*

Have supplies available

There are a number of basic office supplies you will want to have on hand. Here is a checklist of the most important items:

- Hanging folders and manila file folders—plenty of them
- Labels for the folder tabs
- An 8½" x 11" spiral-bound notepad
- Writing utensils for taking notes and writing labels

Make sure these supplies are available when you show up for your appointment with yourself to carry out the purge.

Have boxes ready

Gather four large boxes, and bring them to your appointment. Make sure the boxes are big enough to hold a lot. You will use these to organize items as you pick them up from your desk and other flat surfaces in your office space.

Bring the right attitude to the task

I repeat: this appointment is important. Show yourself the same respect you would show your doctor, your golf pro, your attorney, your boss, your spouse or significant other—and honor your obligation by showing up on time, just as you would show up for your physical exam or your golfing lesson on time.

The objective is to complete the purge as quickly, efficiently, and thoroughly as possible. This is no time for procrastination, no time for putting things off. It is also no time for yielding to distractions. Get it done now, and get it done right—that's the spirit of what we're doing.

Be prepared to feel a little uncomfortable about some of what you are about to do. You will be challenged to disrupt your existing system of organization and information management, and to abandon habits you've come to depend on. You may be reluctant to get rid of some of your items. We are performing a transplant—exchanging one modus operandi that has not served your needs as well as it should, for another that tens of thousands of my clients have found enormously effective.

Let's get started.

> **Be prepared to feel uncomfortable. We are performing a transplant.**

Step One: Purging Your Physical Space

First, make sure you have that spiral-bound notepad handy to write down thoughts, reminders, phone numbers from scraps of paper lying around, and anything else that will help you stay on target. Later, you can transfer all such useful information to appropriate locations in your personal telephone directory or filing system.

Now take the four large boxes you've brought and label them:

- TRASH
- GIVE AWAY/GIVE BACK
- ARCHIVE
- KEEP

Figure 1

When you've labeled the boxes, put them on the floor within easy reach of all the areas where you will be working. We'll come back to them very soon.

Now divide your office or cubicle into areas of focus. For example, you may have the following areas and items:

- Your desktop and computer return
- All drawers, other than file drawers (for example, your desk drawers)
- Table- and countertops, or perhaps a credenza (a piece of office furniture having a long, flat top and sometimes containing file drawers)
- All areas under and around your desk (the floor, for example)
- The near bookcase
- The far bookcase

- Your briefcase
- Your wallet
- Your purse
- File cabinet(s)

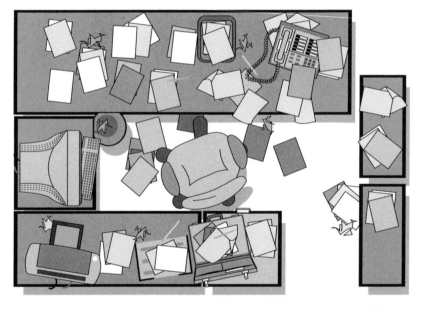

Figure 2

The Famous Seven:
Scissors
Ruler
Stapler
Staple remover
Tape dispenser
Paper-clip holder
Hole-punch

Now, undertake a triage-like operation. Begin at the top of your list and proceed through one area of focus at a time. Start with your desktop. Take each object that you find on your desktop and place it in one of the four boxes—*except for papers* (see next paragraph). That includes what I call the "Famous Seven" desk utensils—your scissors, ruler, stapler, staple remover, tape dispenser, paper-clip

FREQUENTLY ASKED QUESTION
What, exactly, do the labels on the boxes mean?

There is nothing complicated about these labels. What goes into the TRASH box you will throw away. Create a separate box if you have recyclables. And why not recycle? We all know it's good for the environment, and most of us get a feeling of satisfaction from knowing we've done our bit to save trees and help preserve the beauty of our world.

The GIVE AWAY/GIVE BACK box is for items you will give to the Salvation Army, Goodwill, or individuals who might be able to use them. This box is also for items that belong to someone else and need to be returned—that financial report you borrowed from Hank two months ago, the client file that belongs with Marianne. And let's not overlook the four extra staplers you discovered during the purge.

The ARCHIVE box is for information of no practical value whatsoever at this time or in the future, but must be retained for documentation or government-related purposes. Perhaps your company has a central or offsite location for storing these documents and records.

In the KEEP box you will put all items you want or need, for whatever purpose.

If you fill a box, add another with the same label; do not, however, separate the contents of any box into subcategories. For example, don't designate one KEEP box for client data and another for project data. You'll understand why as we go on.

holder, and hole-punch—which should logically go in the KEEP box, unless you have extras of these to give away or borrowed items to be returned to their rightful owners. You don't have to move the telephone or anything else that is connected by wires and in a fixed position.

What to do with papers

Pile all papers and files in one central stack. Do not read them at this time.

When you have them all in one stack, go through them one at a time—quickly—and separate them into the appropriate boxes. Put papers you need to keep in the KEEP box, papers to give back or give away into the GIVE AWAY/GIVE BACK box, and so on. I repeat: go through the papers one at a time; *don't just pick up a bundle and toss it into one of your four boxes.*

Make good use of the TRASH box, and do not categorize, organize, or discriminate among your KEEP items.

The objective is to be efficient and complete. Make good use of the TRASH box! With KEEP items—even non-paper items—do not stop to categorize, organize, or discriminate; take one quick look at what the item is, make your decision, and move on. Remember, this is triage! Quick action is mandatory.

Get rid of it!

Now here's the instruction that requires discipline: *You must get rid of the following items:*

- All trays, except for one *empty* one that will be used as your Out-Tray.

FREQUENTLY ASKED QUESTION
Get rid of my trays? Are you serious?

You may ask, "Why do I have to get rid of my trays? That's where I keep a lot of my papers. What will I do with the information that's in the trays?"

The answer to the second question is simple: Put this information in one of your four labeled boxes. If the papers from your trays don't qualify as trash, give away/give back, or archive materials, then obviously they belong in the KEEP box for now.

The first question—why do you have to get rid of your trays—calls for a brief explanation. Trays and standing file folders are number one among the Black Holes of information. Stacked trays simply serve to transform horizontal chaos into vertical chaos. Your purpose is to eliminate all paths to chaos, and this is one.

Remember this saying: *"Have tray, will fill."* A tray will suck papers into it faster than you realize—and you will have lost control over those papers. The mere presence of a tray, a standing file folder, or anything else that might be a catch-all tempts us to throw a document in it that does not belong there. Get rid of them all, except for one that you will later use as your Out-Tray. Fear not; others who have gone before you will attest to the wisdom of this technique.

No matter how well-intended, systems of organization that rely on trays do not work. The principle here is that, to be efficient, your system of organization must be easy to maintain mentally. Be kind to your brain; you need it for more important uses.

- All standing file folders.
- All loose reminders, such as Post-It notes that you've stuck on your workspace surfaces.

Note: This does not mean Post-Its and paper-clipped notes you've attached to files or documents as reminders of what's in the files. What I'm talking about are the stickies decorating the frame of your computer monitor, your desk lamp, or whatever. You don't really believe those "stickies" are art, do you? If they contain important information, write it down on your notepad.

- All calendars other than your primary one.

Note: This includes any small daily calendars, and any additional calendars except for ones you keep purely for decoration (that is, you don't write on them). Designate one calendar as primary; this may be a paper calendar book or an electronic calendar on your computer or PDA. Transfer all important data to your primary calendar, and *use it exclusively.*

The same goes for desk-pad calendars. Your desk pad is fine as long as it isn't a calendar. If you've written any phone numbers, appointments, memos, or other bits of information on your desk pad, transfer them to your notepad now and your electronic or paper system later.

If you use your desk pad for doodling, resolve right now to break the habit. Get yourself a separate pad of unlined paper for your doodling. That will keep your desk pad clear. A clear desk pad is not just aesthetically pleasing; it also serves as a subconscious reminder that your objective is to keep your physical space free of clutter and messiness. If you have never used a desk pad and see no particular need for one, fine. I'm not advising you to go out and get one.

The difference between TRASH and ARCHIVE

Sometimes it seems as though there's a fine line between trash and archival material. Archival material, as I define it, is of no practical value at this time and may never be. However, because it might be needed at some future time for documentation purposes, government purposes, or legal reasons, it must be archived. Ask yourself this question: might this material be necessary someday for documenting my company's practices, or my own?

You may or may not know the answer to that question. If you do, then go with your answer. If you don't know whether or not the material might need to be kept, ask someone who does know before putting it in the TRASH box. For more on archival materials, see page 97.

Leave a space on your desktop

One last thing about purging your desktop: when you've got it completely cleared, designate a space for collecting incoming material. This will be your Virtual In-Tray. The space should be 8½" x 11" so that incoming files and other working material can "land" on it—but *it must* not *be a physical tray*. It is only a space on your desk that you will always keep free.

This space should be in the lower-right or lower-left corner of your desk. "Lower" means nearest you as you sit at your desk. Choose left or right corner according to which is closer to your door or entrance-way so that whenever someone brings you

> Designate a space in the lower-right or lower-left corner of your desk to receive incoming material.

an item, the person will easily see where to put it. Technique #3 will be about setting up and using the Virtual In-Tray; for now, just register the space in your consciousness and keep it clear on your desk.

Positive items for your desk

Now you may put back on your desk objects that you enjoy having within your view: photos of family, friends, or pets, for example. Also put back your other important working objects, such as your calculator and your PDA or paper organizer. Make sure these tools, as well as your desk lamp and telephone, are in sensible, reachable positions. By all means, display your diplomas, awards, or certificates of achievement. These should be hung on your wall. And why shouldn't you have them on display? You've worked hard for them. Show them off proudly.

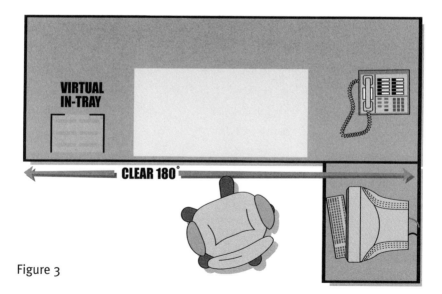

Figure 3

Moving along...

Now that you've finished with your desktop, move on to the next area in your sequence. You're on a roll. If you have a computer return, that would be the next logical space to purge. Remove all the odds and ends that have collected in that space—pencils, notepads, books, Post-It notes, Zip and floppy disks, and so forth.

Continue doing this, one area after another. Finish cleaning off all exposed, flat surfaces—desktop, return, credenza, the tops of your bookcases and tops of your file cabinets (don't forget them!) and the floor. Use the list of spaces on pages 21 and 22 as a checklist to make sure you purge every surface. Be sure to purge your wallet or purse, as well as your briefcase.

You will quickly see that I am understating the scope of this process. What I just said takes up only one paragraph, but if you've accumulated a monster-sized mess, the task could take a while. Just do it, and do it thoroughly! This clean-up is fundamental to achieving your purpose.

Finally, go out to your car. Inspect it thoroughly. Front seat, back seat. Front-seat floorwell, back-seat floorwell. Under the seats. Glove compartment. Door panel compartments. If it's a sedan, check the ledge behind the rear seat. If it's a sports car, check the jump seat area. And finish up with the trunk or cargo space. Clean out the trash. Take everything that belongs in your office back inside, and deposit it all in the appropriate boxes. Make your car as organized and comfortable as your office space. You will find it easy to keep it that way. Your clean car will reinforce the new behavior pattern you're developing.

> Your clean car will reinforce the new behavior pattern you're developing.

Now Take a Breather

Your workspace is looking great. Did you ever imagine you could be occupying such an organized work environment? Now you have those four boxes full of items and information still in the middle of the floor. We'll take care of them shortly.

Enjoy this moment. Look around yourself, and heave a sigh of satisfaction. You'll be getting back to work on the rest of the purge in a few minutes.

Step Two: Set Up a Library

It's time to set up what I call your Library, an easily accessible place to keep such items as newspaper clippings and trade journal articles containing information you're likely to need later. All that's needed is an adequate amount of space in a file drawer, plus a supply of hanging folders and manila file folders.

The instructions for setting up your Library are simple:

- Designate an area in one of your filing cabinets to keep Library items. This can be a particular drawer, two drawers, or however much space you'll need.
- Outfit the area with hanging folders and manila file folders.
- Label the folders as soon as you put content into them.

Step Three: Empty Those Boxes

Look around your workspace. The only items cluttering your view should be the four boxes you created to hold your purged materials. And now it's time to deal with them. Let's do so in this order:

1. TRASH/RECYCLING
2. GIVE AWAY/GIVE BACK
3. ARCHIVE
4. KEEP

First, take your trash and recycling to your company's central trash and recycling area. The point is to *do it yourself.* Believe me, you will feel good. Nothing can get a load off your mind better than getting a load out of your office and experiencing the sublime pleasure of disposing of it yourself. Physically.

Next, disperse the items in your GIVE AWAY/GIVE BACK box. Start with those items you've borrowed from other people. Take them all back to their rightful owners or caretakers. If you are too embarrassed about returning some items—you still have that 1999 annual report that belongs to Dorothy, for example—leave it on her chair when she's not in. Just get all of these items back without delay.

If you have items for the Goodwill, Salvation Army, or any other outside recipient, leave them in the box. Place the box containing those items beside your door so you remember to take them out when you leave. Plan to deliver them to the appropriate recipient today, if possible. *Do not put this off.*

Now take the items in the ARCHIVE box to their proper storage locations. For more about archives, see page 82.

> **Taking your trash and recycling out yourself will make you will feel good.**

Now turn to your KEEP box. Take a deep breath, because this is the one that will require you to think most clearly. I'm going to have you empty the KEEP box in several steps, and we'll give them each a new "Step" number.

Step Four: Put Your Desk Utensils Where They Belong

You have probably gathered an assortment of desk tools in the KEEP box. Put all of them in your top left or top right desk drawer.

Note: I am suggesting the top left or right drawer because, in most desks, these are usually deep enough to hold such objects as your tape dispenser, if you have one, and other items that won't fit in a shallower drawer. If you have a center drawer, it might be too shallow to hold some common desk utensils.

I highly recommend using a drawer organizer that will fit this space and hold your Famous Seven—your scissors, ruler, stapler, staple remover, tape dispenser, paper-clip holder, and hole-punch. If you don't have a drawer organizer, go to the nearest office supply store and pick one up.

Always keep your utensils in this location for instant accessibility.

Step Five: Purge Your Active and Personal Paper Files

It is time to attack the immediate paper-based files that you work with. As you follow this step, you will establish a system by which you can eventually do all of your filing. But concentrate, for the time being, on a small number of special files, typically those that are your most active—files that would naturally go into the bottom-left or bottom-right filing drawer of your desk.

Your primary system of paper filing should use hanging folders with one or more manila file folders inside each hanging folder. Make sure you have an ample supply of empty hanging and manila file folders within reach.

Follow these steps:

1. Sort through the files and documents you've placed in the KEEP box, and pull out everything that meets *any* of the following criteria:

   - You're actively in and out of these files throughout the day.
   - They are confidential.
   - They contain personal files, for example those regarding car, health, or life insurance policies that you can only deal with during working hours.

   Leave all other files and papers in your KEEP box for now.

2. Choose the drawer in your desk to hold these files. If there are a lot of them, you may need to use both the bottom-right and the bottom-left drawers.

> **Use hanging folders with one or more manila folders inside.**

3. Clean out the drawer(s). If there are any desk utensils inside, put them in the drawer with your Famous Seven. Sort through all files that you pull out of the drawer. Put files and papers that do not meet any of the above criteria in the KEEP box. Put files that *do* meet the criteria—they are active, personal, or confidential—together with those you've just separated out.

4. Establish the concept by which you will organize all of your active work files and make tabs for your hanging folders corresponding to that concept. I recommend organizing your files by either Client, Project, or Task. Don't worry about subfolders for now. Thus, if you organize your files by Client, make tabs with the names of your clients, for example Abbot Construction, Bainbridge Island Associates, and so on.

FREQUENTLY ASKED QUESTION

This way of organizing files doesn't really fit my work. Can I use some other method?

It is my experience that the Client, Project, or Task method will best serve your interests and make your filing strategy easier. I realize, however, that some companies and organizations have their own filing standards, and I certainly do not want you to go against the grain. Assuming that you are free to determine your own filing method, though, I would encourage you to give mine a fighting chance.

Note: You will be using the same system for the materials you keep in your filing cabinet. (We'll get to that in Step Six, below.)

5. Take the files and papers you're working on and file them according to this scheme. *Make sure all folders are labeled now.* You do not want to come back later and have to figure out what content is in which folder.

Step Six: Empty the Rest of Your KEEP Box

Now sort through the remaining papers and files in your KEEP box. There may still be a lot of them, so take another deep breath and plunge in.

If you use a system of filing different from the one we've discussed—that is, not based on the Client, Project, or Task concept—I urge you again to try my recommendation. In any case, be sure to use the same concept for organizing the files in your filing cabinet that you use for those in your desk drawer.

You are still working only with the files and papers you've gathered in the KEEP box. *Do not take anything out* of your filing cabinet at this time. Instead, use fresh hanging folders and manila file folders in your filing cabinet. Label them appropriately for the files and papers in your KEEP box. We'll talk about what to do with the old folders shortly.

Now take each item from the KEEP box and put it in the appropriate new file folder. As before, do this one item at a time. If you find items that belong in your Library, put them there and be sure to label them. Place these files in the filing cabinet where they belong for instant retrievability.

> **Use the same concept for organizing in your filing cabinet and your desk drawer.**

Follow these principles:

- *Every file and document has its place.* Do not leave any "orphan files" or loose documents lying around.
- Use a combination of manila file folders and hanging folders. Reserve hanging folders for holding several manila file folders with related content.
- Again, do not put off labeling files and folders. Label everything as you file it.

Now go through all of your old folders. Keep those that are still relevant, and move all files from unnecessary folders into the appropriate new folders. As a hypothetical example, if you've created a new Client folder named "Acme Freight," move all documents pertaining to Acme

Freight into that folder. The same procedure applies if you use Project or Task as your organizing concept. Your goal is to have every file located where you can readily find it within its appropriate Client, Project, or Task folder.

Active work items

Any items that you need to work on in the near future should be placed on your credenza or work table (separate from your desk). We'll come back and organize this functional space in Technique #5, but for now, just make sure that you place these particular items in a single stack.

Phone messages? Memos? Random bits of information?

Earlier, I asked you to get rid of loose reminder slips. However, if you still find chits of paper containing information you've hastily scribbled; if you have "While You Were Out" phone messages or other such notes; if you have loose memos with important contact information on them—this is your chance to save the information.

Gather all of this material together and sort it. Put all of your phone messages in one stack and set them aside for now. We'll return to them for our last task today.

Take all other slips of paper, and write down on your notepad all the information you need to keep. For now, don't be too concerned with organizing the information; just make sure you will be able to read your notes later, when we come back to integrate the information into your working system.

Use your wastebasket or shredder for each piece of paper once you've transferred the information to your notepad.

Guess what? Your boxes are empty!

When you've finished this step, there should be nothing left in the KEEP box. Hooray! You've cleaned out the boxes, and that means you've cleaned up your office space!

And it means you've done all there is to do for now. You've mastered Technique #1. Congratulations!

Now if this first technique seemed a big one, take heart. The remaining techniques are not as complex. Don't be afraid to move on to the rest. It all gets easier from here. Meanwhile, I'd say you deserve a break. Go home. Go for a walk. Or at least do something that relaxes you. And be proud of what you've accomplished.

TECHNIQUE #2:
Workspace Layout
Increase the open space in your work area and create an atmosphere of efficiency

Purging your workspace was the essential first step toward maximizing your productivity. The next logical step is to make sure your office is set up for efficient information processing. In this chapter, I'm going to show you the best way to organize your space. Perhaps your office or cubicle is already laid out in that way. If it isn't, I urge you to reorganize your furnishings.

Like the purge described in Technique #1, reorganizing your workspace may require you to change your way of thinking about certain things—the physical layout of your desk and other office furniture. You will see, though, that it's a *positive* experience, and once you have applied Technique #2, you will begin to see its utility.

Being Proactive in a Reactive World

Being proactive in a reactive world. Have you ever heard this phrase? Our world seems to hurl things at us faster than we can think. Life sometimes seems to be an unending cacophony of simultaneous demands: "Answer Harry's email message. Return Emma's call. Kim wants that report right now. Jamie needs to see you a.s.a.p."

How do you handle it? How do you act proactively to take control of your life when you have to *react* to so many demands coming from all sides?

The first thing you need to do is to create an atmosphere of efficiency—eliminate obstacles that can keep you from working at the peak of your abilities. You need to set up a working environment that gives you a positive, confident outlook, facilitates your workflow, and puts you in charge of setting priorities.

Efficiency has two components, physical and psychological. The techniques you are learning in this book will maximize both your physical efficiency and your mental or psychological efficiency. The physical layout of your workspace centers on a set of organizational tools that I have developed. These will enable you to process your workflow quickly, and once you absorb my method and system, you will be able to dispatch incoming information automatically.

> Being proactive in a reactive world requires you to create an atmosphere of efficiency.

Hence, the psychology behind your office environment: Your new workflow-processing techniques will encourage you to form positive habits. You will quickly see your performance improve, and your positive feelings will encourage you to repeat the techniques—because they work! Soon you will have developed a new pattern of working behavior.

And remember, that's why you're reading this book: You're hoping to change the way you work. You want to work smarter. You want to increase your productivity and reduce your stress.

Desk Position and Workspace Layout

In recent decades, research on the mind has led to methodologies for achieving greater focus and concentration, and yet my experience in consulting at many corporations tells me we have paid little attention to the spatial layout of our workspaces to support focus and concentration. Distractions abound, and old patterns still govern office and workspace layout regardless of whether or not they contribute to working efficiency.

Spatial layout is important to how you work. Understand, though, that we are not talking about interior design. I'm not telling you to spend weeks looking at photos and drawings, scaling them out, and reviewing them in a committee. For

> Spatial layout is important to how you work.

me, *spatial layout* is walking into a room; looking at the placement of the desk relative to the doorway and other people who may work in the same room; seeing where the computer, guest chairs, and other furniture are located; and then determining whether or not all elements are in their most appropriate places.

Be open to change

For a great many people, change is easy in concept but difficult in application. When I practice my consulting business, I very often have to twist clients' arms (figuratively, of course) to reorganize their office layout. They may have spent years in the same office and have grown comfortable with it as it is. The feel of your workspace is important; you can't work efficiently in an environment that seems out of kilter. On the other hand, you also can't work efficiently in an office that's not designed for efficiency. However you feel about your current office space, the absolute, number one criterion about its layout must be that it *supports you in working effectively and creatively.*

A lot of office set-ups don't meet that test. The desk may face the doorway, and traffic in the corridor causes distraction. If you face the doorway—especially an open doorway—it is a lot more likely that someone who's just passing by will stick his or her head in and start a conversation. It is also more likely that you will be distracted simply by seeing someone walk by or hearing a conversation taking place in the corridor.

Another problem is that having your desk face the door doesn't make good use of the space in your office. It puts your desk out in the middle of the room. Unless you have a large office, you can easily take up an inordinate amount of the available space when you add file cabinets and bookcases.

And consider also the placement of your guest chairs. People who place their guest chairs across the desk from themselves make their

Figure 4

desk a barrier that gets in the way of communication. Of course, there are those—particularly some managers—who purposely seat their guests across the desk from them, understanding that the barrier can serve to intimidate. It's not what I recommend.

Figure 4 shows the *wrong* way to organize a workspace. Notice that the desk is in the middle of the room, facing the door, and the desk forms a barrier separating the office's occupant from guests.

The remedies to these layout flaws are obvious, as shown in Figure 5.

I strongly recommend a layout similar to the one illustrated in Figure 5. The best position for your desk is against a wall so that when you are sitting down to work, you are actually facing the wall. Your file cabinet and bookcase should also be against a wall. This will open your room and give you much-needed space. You may gain enough space to add a small conference table and chairs.

Aside from your conference area, your guest chair(s) should be in the corner of your room. If you have two guest chairs, place a small

Figure 5

end table between them and put an incandescent lamp on the table. The effect will be one of warmth. You and your guests will feel more comfortable talking with one another.

If you share an office with another person, your desks should each face a wall. That will give you both a sense of privacy.

Some people resist the idea of facing their desk against a wall. They might be concerned that someone will come into the room from behind and startle them. Or they may worry that facing away from the door gives the impression they are trying to avoid others. However, from my many years of supporting clients' successful efforts to increase their working efficiency, I am convinced that facing away from the doorway is essential to achieving total concentration and full focus. When you face away from the door, your focus and concentration increase immensely and your distractions drop dramatically. People passing by your door see that you are busy, and fewer of them are going to drop in simply to shoot the breeze. This in no way means you are creating a barrier to those who need to see you about important matters. When people have a reason to see you, nothing in your office layout will deter them.

> When you face away from the door, your focus and concentration increase and your distractions drop enormously.

If you are a manager, this especially applies to you. Over the years, I have seen how so many managers are plagued by staff who come in, on a minute-by-minute basis, to ask elementary questions about matters they should very well handle themselves.

Facing the wall is not a signal to your staff that you are too busy for them, but it may make them think twice before coming to you with issues they can figure out for themselves. As a side benefit, facing your desk against the wall might help your staff build their own self-confidence. You can make it clear that you are available when they need to see you—and still encourage them to see how much they can do on their own. This brings to mind the familiar proverb: "Give a man a fish and you feed him for a day. Teach a man to fish and you feed him for a lifetime." Managers, you can teach your staff how to fish by providing adequate training and encouraging them to solve their everyday problems, as much as possible, on their own.

Still skeptical?

I'll offer you the same deal I offer my clients who resist the idea of rearranging their office space: take my advice for thirty days, and if you don't see the results in terms of greater concentration and higher productivity, you have my blessing to restore your office set-up back to its original position. My clients generally experience the improvement well within those thirty days, and I think you will, too.

Do you have a credenza?

I recommend that you have a credenza or a work table that is separate from your desk. This is a good place to keep your printer, if you have one of your own, and the credenza or work table will also be an important location for other tools of efficient working, which we will discuss later in this book. The best place for your credenza or work table is behind you as you are sitting at your desk. See Figure 5.

Attractive and efficient

The physical "makeover" of your desk that we have been discussing is important because it creates an immediate environment that is, *and should always remain,* an attractive space where you can do your best work. Now how do you make it an *efficient* space?

The first answer to that question is: *By keeping your desk clear and free of clutter.*

The second, and equally important, answer is: *By understanding that the primary purpose of your desktop is to work on one—and only one—project at a time.* We'll talk about this principle in Technique #8.

The third answer is: *By keeping it free of all baskets, trays, and standing file folders.* Recall the rule from Technique #1: *No trays on your desk.* Remember this, and say it to yourself like a mantra: "Have tray, will fill." The only apparent exception to this rule is the Virtual In-Tray, which we'll discuss as Technique #3—and it is not really an exception, because there is no *physical* tray involved.

Have tray, will fill.

And now it's on to that topic, for the Virtual In-Tray will complete the transformation of your desktop into a space that serves the purpose of maximum efficiency.

TECHNIQUE #3:
Virtual In-Tray
Create a "runway" for all incoming information

In the chapter describing the purge of your office (Technique #1), I asked you to leave a space in the lower-left or lower-right corner of your desk to become your Virtual In-Tray. Every piece of information that comes to your desk asking for your attention will land on the Virtual In-Tray (or "Vin-Tray" for short).

The illustration on page 49 is a drawing that you can use for your Vin-Tray. I recommend that you photocopy it and enlarge it to 8½ by 11 inches, and tape it down at the bottom-left or bottom-right corner of your desk where you have reserved the space for your Vin-Tray.

Once your Vin-Tray is in place, be sure to inform everyone who brings you work items that they are to place the items there.

Your workspace as an airport with terminals

It is useful to think of your workspace as an airport for your workflow, and your Virtual In-Tray as a runway or landing strip. Incoming work items, like aircraft, do not stop after landing on the Vin-Tray; they must immediately go to where they belong in your organizational system. In the case of signed paperwork for a completed project, for example, the item goes into a file cabinet. In the case of a document that requires action on your part, it goes to your active-task stack, a tool that I call the Turtle. I like to call the functional areas of your workspace "terminals," like the terminals of an airport. (See Technique #5, where we explore the function of the Turtle, and Techniques #9 through #12, where we discuss six more workspace terminals.)

Keep the runway clear

Think now about a vital rule of airports: the runway must always be cleared for the next aircraft to land. Imagine yourself coming in to a major airport. Your plane touches down, and the pilot stops abruptly on the active runway without taxiing to a terminal. The doors of the aircraft open for you and the other passengers to deplane. No other aircraft can land safely on the runway as long as yours stands there. What a danger, what an act of foolishness!

Figure 6

VIRTUAL IN-TRAY

Not emptying your Virtual In-Tray will cause you danger of a different sort, and so the rule applies: *your Vin-Tray must be kept clear for the next work item to land.* You are the pilot who taxis incoming items from the "runway" (the Vin-Tray) to their appropriate terminals. That means you have to move anything that lands in your Vin-Tray to its proper terminal *immediately.* Even if you are busy working on something else—a report, an email message—when something lands in your Vin-Tray, you interrupt what you are doing, pick up the new item from the Vin-Tray, identify it, and move it to the terminal where it belongs.

Keep your Vin-Tray clear for the next work item to land.

I am aware that pausing in your work like this might seem counterintuitive; however, it will begin to make sense to you as you establish your new workflow paradigm. Moving that new item from your Vin-Tray is something you will soon be doing with great speed. You won't interrupt your work long enough to lose your concentration. Eventually, you will taxi items from your Vin-Tray to the correct terminal automatically.

In this way, your Virtual In-Tray will always be empty while you are seated at your desk. Of course, while you are away from your desk, people will bring you items, filling your Vin-Tray. Your immediate task, as soon as you return to your desk, is to sort those newly arrived items out and taxi them to their proper terminals. Pick up the items one by one, identify them, and place them where they belong. When your Vin-Tray is empty, return to your present work.

The Vin-Tray on your desk has its counterpart on your computer: your email Inbox. Technique #13, later in this book, is about how to treat your email like your incoming paperwork.

FREQUENTLY ASKED QUESTION
I thought you said I was not supposed to have any trays on my desk. So what's this Virtual In-Tray?

It's not an actual tray, at least not in the physical sense; it's a flat spot on the top of your desk. That's why we call it virtual. But it serves the purpose of an in-tray as far as being the place where incoming items arrive. Unlike physical trays, however, nothing remains in the Vin-Tray.

By making it a virtual tray, we eliminate the temptation to accumulate items in it that don't belong there. Actually, nothing stays in the Vin-Tray—everything that lands there is on its way to a terminal. Like an airplane on the landing strip.

Not "What is it?" but "Where does it go?"

One important principle to learn is that you should not determine what to do with an item based on what it is; rather, you make that determination based on where it belongs in your workflow organization system. You don't handle a paper file one way, a brochure or a fax or a letter another way, and an email message yet another way. All of these, when they reach your workspace, require your attention; the crucial way of defining them is by where they go in your new organizing system. Essentially, you determine an item's identity by the terminal you will put it into.

To state this another way, when you receive a work item, the first thing you do is to consciously disregard its form—a file, a flow chart, a letter, a mock-up for a brochure, and so on—and think of which terminal it goes to. You will learn my method of making these determinations when you learn Techniques #5 and #9–#12.

When you receive a work item, disregard its form and think of where it goes.

The procedure that routes tangible items through your Virtual In-Tray applies similarly to email and voice-mail. And that brings us to the next technique: how to prepare your computer and voice-mail system for maximum efficiency.

TECHNIQUE #4:
Computer and Voice-mail Purge
Clean up your electronic workspace

Just as you need a clean and efficiently organized physical workspace for achieving your maximum productivity, you need to organize your electronic workspace for top-notch effectiveness. You should never have to spend more than a few seconds locating a crucial computer file; nor should you ever have to wonder where you've kept important email messages.

Computer files and paper files: What's the difference?

Functionally, there's no difference between paper files and your electronic data; however, a lot of people have a harder time keeping their computer files organized. This is because it's so easy to save computer files, and we don't always pay close attention to where a file is located; we click the Save button and we know the file is saved—somewhere. However, after we've closed out of the program we may have to hunt through several folders, or use the computer's Search function, to find that file again. Three weeks pass, and we might not

> In concept, there's no difference between computer files and paper files, but some people have a harder time keeping their computer files organized.

remember the filename or anything else specific enough to help us find it.

Later in this book, we'll describe a technique for systematically saving and naming files. First, however, we need to clear the slate and build in an *electronic* organizational structure in order to make sense of the files and email folders you already have.

Your Document Files and Other Working Files

Because computer files are conceptually the same as paper files, you should think of them as you think of paper files. Your computer files contain relevant documents, project lists and outlines, databases, spreadsheets, designs, graphics, notes to yourself, audio and video materials, and so on. You need them organized in a way that enables you to bring any single file up onto your screen whenever you need it. You do not want to spend precious time trying to figure out where something is, much less lose it completely in the chaos within your software.

The first thing to do in purging computer files is to make sure you have all of your working folders together within one top-level folder. If you're running Microsoft Windows, you can use the folder named My Documents that comes automatically installed in the system. If you prefer—or if you're not using Windows—you can create a top-level folder and name it "My Documents" or, if you prefer, "Filing Cabinet." For the purposes of the present discussion, I'll continue to refer to this top-level folder as "My Documents."

When you have that folder in place, create within it new folders corresponding to the scheme you used for paper files. That is, organize your folders by Client, Project, or Task. See Figure 7 for an example of a system organized by Client.

Frequently Asked Question
In my computer, what's the difference between a *file* and a *folder?*

Computer terminology can sometimes be confusing, but the difference between a *file* and a *folder* can be explained simply.

Files. A computer file is a specific document or software program. When you use your word processor, your spreadsheet program, or another program to create a document and you save the document, the document is saved as a file with a name.

Document files, as opposed to program files, are often called data files. When you save a document in Microsoft Word or Excel, or in Adobe PhotoShop, or Corel Painter, or any other application, you are creating a data file.

Folders. A computer folder is a container for multiple files. Folders are usually symbolized by the image, or icon, of a manila file folder on your computer screen. When you click or double-click on a folder icon, you see the names of files contained by the folder.

Create a folder named "Archive," and use it for storing documents of no relevance except possible future legal, governmental, or documentation reasons.

Tip: If you type a character such as ` (French accent grave) or ~ (tilde) at the beginning of Archive when you're naming the folder, this folder will appear on your screen ahead of all other names in the alphabetical sequence. (See the example `Archive in Figure 7.)

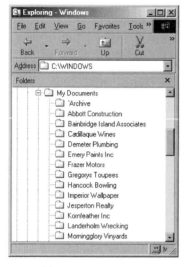

Figure 7

Now go through all of your old document folders and move all existing files and subfolders into the appropriate folders that you've just created. For example, if you've created a Client folder named Abbott Construction (as in Figure 7), move all documents pertaining to Abbott Construction into that folder. Do the same with documents relating to all other clients; that is, move them into the folders where they belong.

The same general procedure applies if you use Project or Task as your organizing concept. Your goal is to have every document in your computer located where you can readily find it within its appropriate Client, Project, or Task folder.

To reach this goal, be sure to open *all* of your old folders—not just those you know contain document files—and move every working file to the folder where it belongs. The reason I'm saying this is because you might discover some stray files in your old folders, files you've lost track of. This is your opportunity to corral them and make sure you'll find them easily the next time you need them.

Move working data files, but not program files, into My Documents.

Do not move program files or folders—those containing the software that runs your applications, such as Microsoft Office, Quicken, PhotoShop, and all other applications. Move only *working data files* into the central folder structure you've just created.

Delete!

While you are organizing your data files, feel free to delete every file that no longer has any value, now or in the future—papers, reports, letters, graphics, PowerPoint slides, worksheets, and so on. Be very careful not to delete any files that should go into the Archive folder.

Archive files

Move all files suitable for archiving into your Archive folder. We'll take up the subject of archiving later in this book, but for now, you can just stick with what I said above: archival content comprises documents that are of no relevance except for possible future legal, governmental, or documentation reasons.

Email Files

Next we turn to email, and I want to begin by asking you a tantalizing question: can you imagine having not one single message in your In-box at the end of every day? Yes, you read that correctly: no messages. Zero, nada, zippo.

Impossible, you say? Well, start imagining it, because I'm going to show you how. That's for Technique #13. Now, though, we have to set up your email program in order for this "daily miracle" to take place.

Most office workers nowadays use Microsoft Outlook, but many others use the America Online (AOL) application, Qualcomm's Eudora, Netscape Mail, or another software product. In certain respects, they all work the same. Whatever email program you use, the first step to getting your message-processing strategy in place is a simple one. Open your email application, and create new folders with the following names:

- Archive
- Clients, Projects, or Tasks (depending on which file-organization approach you use for your other computer files)
- Library/Reference
- Pending (EP)
- Personal
- Reading
- Turtle (ET)

I realize that, if you are reading these pages in sequence, this is the second time you've seen that odd name "Turtle." Please bear with me; I am not assuming you work in a zoo, aquarium, or pet shop. Our friend the Turtle takes center stage when we talk about Technique #5.

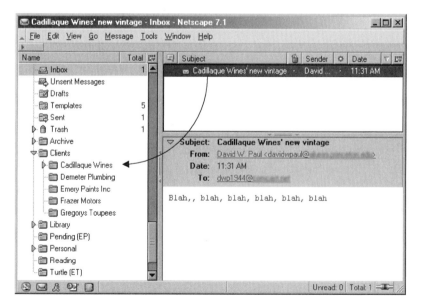

Figure 8

Now go through your old email folders—those where you have all of your saved messages (*not* your In-box)—and move those saved messages into the appropriate new folders. For example, if you have a Client email folder named "Cadillaque Wines," move your saved email from Cadillaque Wines into the Client folder "Cadillaque Wines." If you have a "Sent," "Sent Mail," or "Sent Messages" folder, move those files, too.

Make sure that you move *all* messages out of your old folders.

Note: If you have saved messages that pertain to active work—for example, information pertaining to a report you haven't yet completed—*move these messages into the Turtle (ET) folder.*

Finally, turn to your In-box. Go through those messages one by one, moving them to the appropriate new folders. Move any messages that pertain to active work into the Turtle (ET) folder.

Figure 9

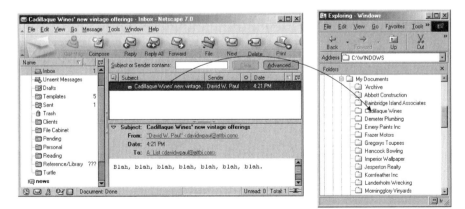

Delete your old folders

Your old email folders should be empty now. You can delete those old folders, for you will not be using them any more. *Do not attempt to delete your "Sent" folder, and do not delete permanent folders such as your Inbox or Trash.*

You have completed the purge of your email. There will be more about processing your email messages later in this book, but for now, take a deep breath and enjoy the satisfaction of having cleaned up your computer filing system.

Voice-mail

If you use voice-mail often, you may have a problem with backlogged messages or, even worse, having your callers unable to leave you a message because your mailbox is full. This is a common problem for people who spend a lot of time at meetings or on the road, but anyone who is busy and overloaded with incoming information can experience voice-mail backlogs. Now is the time to purge this electronic Black Hole.

I recommend using a spiral-bound notebook for logging your phone messages. Start by going through the accumulated paper slips and "While You Were Out" memos you collected while purging your physical space (Technique #1: see page 36.) Copy down the essence of each phone message, along with the caller's phone number, in the notebook.

Next, listen to your accumulated voice-mail messages. Again, copy down the essence of each message into the notebook you're using to log your calls. Be sure you take down all information you will need, and delete each message as soon as you have logged it. You can, of course, ignore any calls that don't require returning. But do this responsibly. Don't avoid calls you know you really should return. It's just not good business practice.

Now prioritize your return calls by assigning numbers to them: Number 1 is the call you plan to return first, Number 2 second, and so on. Do this especially if you have many calls to return.

> It's not good business practice to avoid calls you really should return.

That's all. Your voice-mailbox has been cleared, and you are ready to start returning your calls. We'll talk how to manage your voice-mail on an ongoing basis in further pages of this book, particularly in Technique #14.

End of the Purge

By now you should have completed the purge of both your physical space (Technique #1) and your electronic space. Good job! You've probably spent a lot of time and effort getting to this point. In the pages to come, there are still many techniques for getting more out of your job, yourself, and your life, and yet the end goal may seem some distance away. Rest assured that what you've just done is crucial to gaining control over your working habits. The purge you've completed today will make maintaining organization easier tomorrow. If in the past you've lost letters, papers, files, email messages, and electronic documents to the Black Holes that trap information where you couldn't find it or deal with it expeditiously, consider that problem history.

TECHNIQUE #5:
The Turtle
Prioritize all of your active work, all of the time

As we approach that mysterious creature, the Turtle, you must be thinking it's about time. Okay, I won't keep you in suspense any longer. The reason I call this tool the Turtle is that many years ago, a very dear friend gave me a small metal turtle as a paperweight to be placed on top of all the paperwork I needed to do. During my very first training class, while I was teaching about the single stack holding my active work items, I mentioned that I used a turtle as a paperweight for the stack. Someone in the class thought I was calling the stack the "turtle." I adopted the word, and for decades that is what I've called the ordered stack of papers, files, and folders that comprise my active tasks. "Turtle" is easier to remember than "prioritized, active-task paperwork," don't you think? (And it's cute, too!)

But prioritized, active-task paperwork is what the Turtle is all about. Earlier, I made the point that you must reserve your desktop solely for the project you are working on *now*. Remember the mantra from Technique #2: Your desk is for working on *one* project at a time. That's the project that has your highest, most immediate priority. But what about other work in progress?

The answer is the Turtle, the tool you have for holding active (current) tasks other than the one that has your immediate attention: your

> **The Turtle holds active projects other than the one that has your immediate attention.**

second-highest priority, third-highest, and on down the line. The Turtle is a *prioritized active-task repository for all work items that are less important or less time-critical than the work you're doing at the moment.*

Note: Keep in mind that this is not just today's work; it is all the work you have to do, even if it's due two months from now. If you've got it and it requires your input, it belongs in your Turtle.

As we look more closely at the Turtle, you will see that it is not just a "holding tank," but it also wonderfully serves to prioritize your active tasks.

It's Not a Turtle Literally

The Turtle is a single stack of items that contains work you have to do after you've finished the work you're doing at the moment. You keep the stack in priority order by spending no more than two to three minutes each morning refamiliarizing yourself with your work and reprioritizing it (if necessary). I call this inverting your Turtle, and we'll talk about it when we come to Technique #21.

You don't have to use a metal turtle—or a turtle of any literal sort, and certainly not a live one—but I do recommend that you put some kind of personalized paperweight on top of your Turtle stack to keep the papers in place. It can be anything you'd like to use: the clay model of your child's hand that he or she made at school; a pretty art-glass hemisphere your boss gave you for good performance; or whatever you have that will serve the purpose and provide positive emotional reinforcement.

Where should it be located?

The best place for the Turtle is on your credenza, in the position illustrated in Figure 10. It is behind you as you sit facing your desk—intentionally outside your sightline—yet still within easy reach.

Locating the Turtle behind you is very important. The papers representing your upcoming tasks are removed from your immediate line of vision, freeing your mind for concentrating on the work in front of you: the single project that commands your highest priority now. Think of the old saying, "I've put it on a back burner." The Turtle is your back burner. You will move your Turtle projects, one by one, to

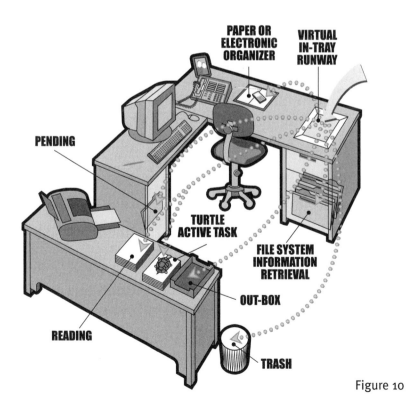

Figure 10

the front burner—your desktop—when you've completed and dispatched what you're working on now.

If you don't have a credenza

The guiding principle about where to keep your Turtle is that it be outside your sightline, yet within easy reach as you sit at your desk. You might put it on a nearby file cabinet, for example. If you have no other alternative, locate the Turtle in a corner of your desktop, preferably outside your peripheral vision and, in any case, as far from the center of your field of vision as possible. The point is to keep your forthcoming tasks out of sight so they don't distract you from what you must do now. This is important from the standpoint of focusing on one project at a time, the subject of Technique #8.

Knock it out

As you become accustomed to using the Turtle, you will discover something valuable: many of your work items can dispatched quickly—especially those little tasks that tempt you to put them aside until some indefinite future time. You will be amazed to see how many small tasks you can knock out as they pop up to the top of the Turtle stack. Even better, you might find you can handle some of them directly from the Virtual In-Tray without even putting them into the Turtle stack.

In fact, this is one key to using your Vin-Tray effectively: a lot of items that land on your desk can be dispatched immediately. Let's say, for example, that you have completed your final review of a contract and now your assistant brings it to you for your signature. Just *pick it up off of your Vin-Tray, sign it, and send it on its way.* If you get a preliminary agenda for an upcoming meeting and you are asked for comments, look it over, make any additions you think are necessary, and send it back. The idea is that you don't want to be filling your Turtle stack with nitpicky work items if you can take care of them quickly and immediately, one at a time. If you perform the task immediately, it might take you only a minute; if you wait and accumulate twenty such tasks, they will seem overwhelming and add to your stress.

Do you know Harry the Hoarder? He's the guy who hoards work. He never handles a task immediately but prefers to set things aside and let them accumulate. Maybe he thinks that heap of papers on his desk makes him look important. In fact, he is holding up the production line, sabotaging other people who need to get on with their work but can't—because Harry is sitting on those items. You definitely don't want to be like Harry.

Prioritizing

Now we come to one of the most important procedures that I can teach you. Your Turtle is meant to hold active tasks in the order in which you will work on them. For each item, you need to know its due date or deadline, and you need to know how far in advance of the due date you must start working on the task. Therefore, just before you place an item in your Turtle, do the following:

- Determine the amount of dedicated time it will take to complete the work.
- At the top of the first sheet, write down the *Completion Date* for this task.
- Count back the number of days you will need to complete the task, and write the *Start Date* at the top of the first sheet, to the left of the Completion Date. Make sure the Start Date is clearly

visible, because you will need to see it at a glance each morning when you look through your Turtle materials.

- *Be diligent about this procedure!* As simple as it seems, it is the key to bringing your workflow under control. The dates you use for your active-task items determine your working priorities. The Turtle is a simple device that keeps you organized and on schedule.

Turtle Holding Area (THA) and Turtle Sheets

The Turtle is a particular stack of papers containing your upcoming work. Now you may be wondering, What if I have a project that consists of a large amount of information? Won't that overwhelm my orderly Turtle stack?

Yes, it will. Here's how to prevent that: if you have a thick or complex work project, such as a book manuscript, a blueprint, or massive tax-accounting files, you create for it a Turtle Holding Area, or THA. Choose a place that's either on a bookshelf, in your closet or vertical storage cabinet, a credenza drawer, or somewhere else that is in your office but away from your desk. You can even designate a specific section within a file cabinet for this purpose as long as you have an empty drawer in

> **Create a Turtle Holding Area (THA) for thick or complex materials, and log the items' location on Turtle Sheets.**

it. Whatever location you choose, reserve that space for active work items that are too big or bulky to put in your Turtle stack.

Now create a Turtle Sheet. This will be a single sheet of paper to keep in your Turtle, which you use to log identifying information about the project you're putting in the THA. Use an 8½" by 11" sheet for *each* such project, and write or type on it the following:

- **Project Title:** A short, descriptive phrase matching, or relating to, the name of the main overarching project.
- **Description:** A description of the active task, brief yet allowing for some elaboration beyond the project title.
- **Estimated Time to Complete:** The total time *you* expect to spend on the task from the moment you start. Be very honest with yourself in making this estimate.
- **Completion Date:** The date the work is due; the deadline. This is the most important field on the Turtle Sheet. The Completion Date determines your start date; that's why you fill it before the Start Date. In addition to setting a due date, the completion date field will be useful when you prioritize your Turtle items.

Hint: Even if a specific task doesn't have a definite deadline, you should give it a completion date according to what works best for you. The date may not be set in stone, but the more seriously you take it, the more likely you are to get it done in a timely fashion—and without stressing out.

- **Start Date:** The date on which you actually begin working on the task. The "Start Date" field assumes that there will be some projects, or portions of a project, that you do not complete in one day.
- **Location of Information Needed:** Where to find information (files or reference materials) you need when working on this project. Such materials might be located in your filing cabinets, on your bookshelves, or outside your office in somebody else's possession. This field on the Turtle Sheet will guide you to them. Keep the "Location of Information" field updated by crossing off materials you have already used and/or no longer need, and by adding the locations of other materials as you realize you need them.

- **Others Involved:** Other people involved in the project, what their roles are, and any information that will help you identify or locate them.
- **To Whom/Where to File After Completion:** Where to deliver the finished task. The information in this field keeps you moving—you don't have to think about what to do with the materials when they are ready to be passed along. It's important to know this, especially when the active task is part of a larger project involving other people or when some time elapses between your receiving the assignment and your completion of it.
- **Hint:** It's a good idea to take a red pen and circle the completion date and the person or place to whom the work is to be delivered, and then draw a line connecting the two. Doing this gives you a visual cue, every time you check the Turtle Sheet, that someone is depending on you to complete the task by a specified date.
- **Notes:** Use this space for ideas that come to mind. For example, if you think of steps involved in completing the project, this is the place to write them down. Don't worry about chronology or sequence—just get those ideas down on paper. You can number their sequence afterward.
- **Today's Date:** The day when you are initially filling out the Turtle Sheet. (Usually this will also be the day when the task first came to your attention.)

The physical reason for using Turtle Sheets is to keep your Turtle stack relatively thin and uncluttered. The psychological benefit is that a single sheet is far less daunting than a thick file, manuscript, bundle of blueprints, or some other bulky item. Taming your Turtle will seem more achievable if the stack is thinner. And having the Turtle Sheet in

TURTLE SHEET

Project title:

Description:

Estimated time to complete:

Completion date: Start date:

Location of information needed:

Others involved:

To whom/where to file after completion:

Notes:

Today's date:

Figure 11

FREQUENTLY ASKED QUESTION
Which fields on the Turtle Sheet are required?

The information you write on the Turtle Sheet is at your discretion; however, I strongly suggest that you fill in at least five fields: the Project Title field, the Completion Date, the Start Date, Location of Information Needed, and Today's Date.

its prioritized place reminds you exactly what the project is and when you need to start the task.

Note: Some of the "graduates" of my training program like to fill out a Turtle Sheet for every item in their Turtle stacks, not just those that are physically stored elsewhere. They staple the Turtle Sheet to the top page of the item. You might find this practice preferable to just writing the completion date and start date on the top sheet of each item. Using a Turtle Sheet gives you more information about each item at a glance.

Additional uses for Turtle Sheets

You might have active tasks for which there is no physical item to hold in the Turtle—no file, document, letter, or anything. The task may center on a computer file that you need to handle onscreen without ever touching a hard copy; an example is a spreadsheet residing on a password-protected company server, open for entries by you and certain other authorized staff members. Or a task might involve physical items held outside your workspace—a model under construction in another office or workroom, or an experiment being performed in a lab, for example. It's a good idea for you to fill out a Turtle Sheet for each such task and place it in your Turtle stack according to its priority.

Another use for a Turtle Sheet is to capture verbal requests you receive. Let's say, for example, that your manager calls you and asks you to write a summary of a meeting you just attended. There won't be a paper or email notice of this new assignment, so you need to record it immediately. Use a Turtle Sheet for this exactly as you would for any other task you must complete.

And let's not forget about how many terrific ideas you have that just spring out of your mind. The Turtle Sheet is the net that captures those great ideas and gives you the tool to bring them to fruition. I keep Turtle Sheets in my briefcase, in my glove compartment, and on my bed stand. (You know that you have had some of your most brilliant ideas when awakening abruptly at 3:00 a.m.) If you are old enough to know what a grease pencil is, I keep one in my shower to write with on the tile. Laugh if you will, but I get a lot of good ideas while showering—and I don't lose any of them to lapses of memory.

What to Do Now

While we were emptying your KEEP box, I asked you to place all papers and files that require your attention on your credenza or work table, or in some other place separate from your desk. Now it's time to return to those papers—your active tasks—and make a Turtle stack from them. If some are large, bulky, or complex materials, place them in your Turtle Holding Area and log the pertinent information about them on Turtle Sheets, including, of course, their location (THA).

> Don't use your Turtle for active projects that are awaiting input from someone else. Those tasks go to Pending.

FREQUENTLY ASKED QUESTION
How thick or bulky should work materials be for me to consign them to the THA?

As a rule of thumb, I tell my clients that any piece of work thicker than five sheets should go into the Turtle Holding Area (THA). The objective is to keep a contained stack of work in your Turtle. When you turn around from your desk and glance at the Turtle, you should not feel stressed by the size or thickness of the stack. You should be able to say to yourself with confidence, "Yes, that is a manageable amount of work. I can handle it."

Decide the priority of the work, and place the item of highest, or most immediate, priority on the top of the stack, with its Start Date clearly visible. Arrange all other items in descending order of priority from top to bottom. Be sure to include Turtle Sheets representing work in your THA.

One more important point: If any of your current work projects are awaiting input from someone else—or if you cannot complete them because some scheduled event must take place first—*do not put these items in the Turtle stack.* The best location for them is another terminal, called "Pending," which will be discussed as Technique #10.

Front of Your Head, Back of Your Head

Earlier, we talked about front-burner projects and back-burner projects. You know by now that the proper working procedure has only one task on the "front burner"—your desk—at a time. That is your number one priority, your immediate assignment. All other active tasks are in your Turtle, on the "back burner," arranged in priority so that you will know what you are to work on when you've finished your current task.

Do you see the beauty in this? Do you feel the liberating force? The Turtle is behind you as you sit facing your desk, out of your sightline. "Out of sight, out of mind"—this old saying, usually used negatively, has a positive meaning in our situation; those upcoming tasks are no longer looming over you, within sight, and you don't have them rattling around in the back of your head as you work on your top-priority task. You don't worry about the deadlines associated with them. You're free to focus your attention fully on what is in front of you. That is what receives your full creative energy, and you will work on it at your peak efficiency.

You've driven up the entrance ramp and are now on the road to maximum productivity. Full speed ahead!

Completing the "Productivity Makeover" of Your Workspace

Let's move on from the basics to some further changes in your physical workspace. These changes will add to the efficiency of your office and help you improve your working habits. Put them into practice, and you will see your productivity increase by several more notches.

TECHNIQUE #6:
"Clear 180"
Focus and concentrate on a whole new level

Earlier in this book, we talked about the importance of keeping your desktop neat and free of trays. Now I'd like to extend that discussion by explaining why it is important to maintain a "clear 180."

By "180," I mean the 180 degrees of your sightline from periphery to periphery as you sit at your desk facing forward. A "clear 180" means there is nothing within that sightline that distracts you from your work. All you see are materials relating to the task on which you are currently working, plus your telephone, your appointments calendar or PDA, and a few positive items that you enjoy having within your view, such as family pictures or photos of your pets.

Let's think again about the reasons for having no trays on your desk. Besides the fact that trays are one of the Black Holes of information that suck in documents, memos, letters, and other materials that you need to find readily, they are also an eyesore and a distraction. You don't want them anywhere in your 180 where they can grab your attention away from the job you're attending to.

So, too, with any other objects that might disturb your focus. The important principle

> **The 180 of your environment should be an attractive space that enables you to do your best work.**

about your 180 is to give it a positive, reinforcing air. As you develop your new working habits, you will want to keep clutter and unwanted objects out of your space. You want this space—the area you are looking at whenever you are at your desk—to contain items that promote positive experiences for you. That way, you can really focus in on the work at hand.

For an illustration of the area described by the clear 180, see Figure 3 on page 28.

TECHNIQUE #7:
Computer Placement
Locate your computer where it will serve you best

W here should your computer be? Many people have their computer on their desk. However, that's not the best place for it. Why? Because on your desk, it sabotages your clear 180.

Your computer belongs on your *computer return*. The return is a square or rectangular table connected to your desk at the left or right, forming an L shape. (See Figure 12.) Ideally, the return has a sliding tray underneath your monitor that holds your keyboard. Your central processing unit, or CPU, will usually go under the return alongside your leg, although if it is a flat unit (as opposed to a "tower" unit) it can also rest under the monitor to give the monitor more height. If you have an all-in-one computer, such as the Apple iMac or eMac, or use a laptop or notebook computer in your office, the monitor and CPU are all in one piece, sitting compactly on top of your return.

The computer return is a marvelous piece of furniture. It gives you a horizontal surface that is reserved for your computer, off to the side of your desk and out of your 180.

If you don't have a computer return
If your furnishings don't include a computer return, your computer may go on your credenza, assuming you have one. Make sure the

credenza is at the right height and has enough leg room that you can work comfortably and ergonomically.

You might consider asking your manager to procure a computer return for you. After all, good office furniture is not a luxury; it's an aid to your working efficiency, and it's good for your health. It's in your manager's interest to have you working at your best and avoiding painful stress injuries that are sometimes caused by poor ergonomics.

If you don't have enough space in your office for either a return or a credenza, then you obviously have to keep your computer on your desk. Just make sure that you keep it toward one end of your desk—*as far to the edge of your 180 as is practical.* It may be on the right edge of your 180 or the left. This will allow you to keep much of your 180 clear.

The computer return is a marvelous piece of furniture. Ask your manager to get you one.

Figure 12

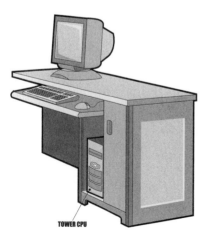

TOWER CPU

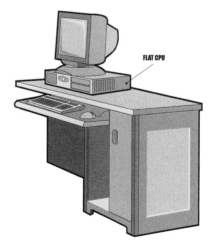

FLAT CPU

TECHNIQUE #8:
Focus on One Project at a Time
The last word on your desktop

Before picking up *The Instant Productivity Toolkit*, how often did you think about your desktop? I mean, *really* think about it—its functions, its appearance?

For a lot of people, their desk is a storage facility. Not just the drawers, but the top surface as well. They use their desktop as a convenient parking place for piles and piles of "stuff."

If that's how you've used yours, consider that over. Done. *Finito*. If you applied Technique #1, you cleared everything off your desktop. If you paid attention to Techniques #2 and #7, you were reminded over and over again to keep your desktop free and clear for current work. You learned that even your Virtual In-Tray is to be kept open. A clear 180—that was the explicit point of Technique #6. No trays, no stacks, no piles.

A tool for one project at a time

Have you ever thought about your desktop as a *tool*? I want you, from this day forth, to use your desktop as a tool for working on *one project at a time*. Not two. Not three. *One project*.

> **Your desktop is for working on *one* project at a time.**

FREQUENTLY ASKED QUESTION

Look, I want people to understand that I have a lot of responsibilities. They get that impression when they see plenty of work on my desk. I can keep the items neat and separate. What's the harm in that?

Let's back up and approach this question from another angle. What it seems to be saying is that there are advantages to being *dis*organized: The more papers, files, and memos I have around me, the busier I look. The busier I look, the more important I appear to others. Another advantage, according to this logic, might be that if I appear to be overworked, people are not likely to pile additional work onto me.

In response to that, first of all I would ask, is this really how you want to be? Do you truly believe the *image* of what you do is more important than *what you actually do?* I doubt it. Consider the price you pay for keeping up appearances: there's no satisfaction at doing your job well, no sense of achievement. People whose *modus operandi* is impressing others with their smoke-and-mirrors act sooner or later blow their cover. They're playing a dangerous game for high stakes—stakes that could mean their job.

You want to do your work efficiently, and with more creativity and innovation. From my experience, the best way to start is to set up your working area so that you can focus your concentration on one task at a time, get it done expeditiously, and move on to the next task.

Okay, you might say, no clutter. But why is it necessary to use the desktop for only one project?

Let's consider a parable, of sorts. Forget reality for a moment and imagine yourself in this situation: You are skiing down your favorite slope, a steep slope with many moguls, and you're concentrating intensely on every twist and rise. Suddenly, up ahead and just off the ski path, you see a mountain lion eyeing you from the edge of a wooded area. Now what happens to your concentration?

Chances are, you tumble into a snow bank and hope that mountain lion has already had enough to eat today. So what's the moral?

Back to reality—your workspace—and an interpretation of the parable. The ski slope represents a project you're working on, and the mountain lion represents papers and files left over from yesterday and passively awaiting your attention. You know you should be concentrating on your current project, but there's that stack of other work sitting there, waiting to attack you.

Those papers and files don't belong on your desk. They need to be out of your immediate sight line. You want to keep your eyes on the task that's your immediate objective. Any other work materials within view will pull your attention away from the project you need to be focusing on. Your concentration will be broken. You'll get back to work on the priority project, but then you'll be distracted again by the other work on your desk. This will repeat itself over and over. On a subconscious level, every paper or folder on your desk will be flying up at you like radiation.

That is why it's so important to think of your desk, always, as a place to work on *one project at a time.* That project might be an invoice, a balance sheet, a letter, a memo, a report, a spreadsheet...whatever. Stay with it; focus on it until you've finished it.

But what about multitasking?

Twenty years ago, the word "multitasking" didn't exist; today you see and hear it everywhere in the business world. The assumption is that an employee who can "multitask" is more productive than one who cannot. Job ads and notices call for applicants skilled at multitasking. Managers tell team workers they must be able to multitask. Most people I run into believe they are able to do it and it is necessary to getting their work done.

Personally, I am a disbeliever. The important thing to recognize is that when you are attempting to multitask—and the operative word is *attempting*—you are asking your singular brain to focus on two or more assignments simultaneously. You are expecting yourself to give each of them one hundred percent concentration. It doesn't take Einstein's great-grandchild to figure out that this is impossible. Consider the mathematics: how can you give Project A one hundred percent of your mental energy when you're giving one hundred percent to Project B? The simple truth is that you're giving them each fifty percent *at most*.

Some years ago, there was an interesting IBM commercial on television: A man standing at a whiteboard had a marker in each hand. In his left hand he was redrawing the Mona Lisa from memory, and with his right hand he was writing an intricate mathematical equation. The Mona Lisa was a perfect copy, and the equation looked elegant. If you can draw the Mona Lisa while writing a complicated math equation, you can multitask. I, however, am humble enough to admit I can't do that, so I cannot multitask.

When you're asked to do a number of things and they're all coming at you at once, you probably feel an urge to take them all on at once: to multitask. But the person who can do every task simultaneously—and do them all well—is very, very rare.

The challenge is to deal with information so that you can manage it in a way that avoids having to multitask, or, more accurately, avoids the *attempt* to multitask. This means giving your full attention to one task at a time. Do it to your utmost capability, do it in a timely fashion, and then tackle the next-priority item on your Turtle stack. You might just find that the amount of time it takes you to complete Project A plus the time it takes you for Project B equals less total time than what it would take you to "multitask" them simultaneously. And I don't doubt that you will do them both better.

So what do you tell your manager? What do you say during a job interview? Go ahead, fudge the issue. Tell them, "Yes, I can multitask." Just don't tell them you *will* multitask. The results will speak for themselves when your work exceeds expectations for accuracy and timeliness.

TECHNIQUE #9:
Trash, Out-Tray, and File System
Process your work and keep files instantly retrievable

In earlier chapters, we used an airport metaphor for processing your workflow efficiently. The Virtual In-Tray is the runway on which your work-related information lands, and from there you immediately taxi the incoming materials to terminals where they will be processed in due time. (See, especially, page 47.) Technique #9 is about using three of the terminals to keep files and other information materials organized: Trash, your Out-Tray, and your File System.

Outside the context of our airport metaphor, it might seem odd to refer to these functional objects in your office as "terminals," but it will soon become apparent why the term fits them. These three terminals—Trash, Out-Tray, and File System—have in common the fact that they receive items that do not require further action on your part; they are items you either throw away, pass along to someone else, or file away for instant retrievability.

Let's look at these three terminals, and their functionality as I want you to employ them, one by one.

Trash

Trash seems so uncomplicated: what you don't need or want, you throw away. And yet there are people who have a hard time eliminating trash from their lives. Maybe their mom threw out their comic-book collection before they were ready to part with it. Maybe it was their childhood task to take out the garbage every night, even during an arctic blizzard, and they shiver just thinking about it. They simply find it hard to throw anything away.

Whether that applies to you or not, you need to get rid of your trash promptly. Trash clutters up our desks, our filing cabinets, our floors. It can prevent us from focusing and utilizing our creativity. When our working environment is cluttered, our minds are cluttered and our best qualities, our best work, cannot be realized.

> When our working environment is cluttered, our minds are cluttered.

Calling it a "terminal" does not mean we need to complicate Trash. You can use a standard wastebasket; nothing special is required. Just make sure to keep it in an easy-to-reach place; for example, the position suggested in Figure 13.

Hard to throw away?

There are people who love tossing things out, and then there are pack rats. Most of us fall somewhere between these categories, but if you are one who has a hard time throwing things away—and you know who you are—try asking yourself the following questions about every item:

- *Do I need this for my work, or for tax, legal, documentation, or other archival reasons?* If the answer is no, toss it.

Technique #9 **91**

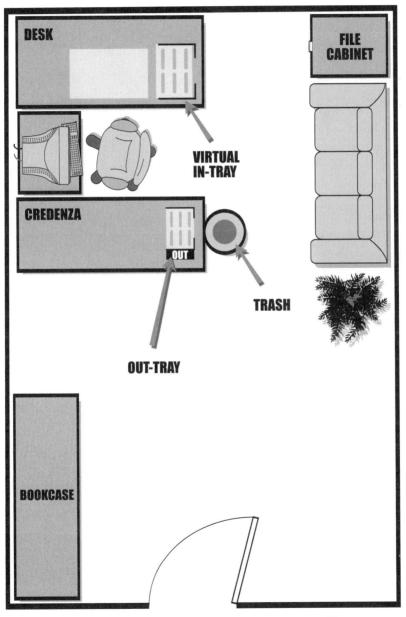

Figure 13

- *Do I foresee a* specific *need for it?* If you think, "Hmm, maybe someday it might be useful," but you can't think how, then take a deep breath and toss it.
- *Does a copy of this item exist somewhere else that's easily accessible?* If you or a colleague might need the item and it exists in a file stored on the company network, on the Internet, or in another easily accessible location, toss it.

Still can't decide? Try this rule of thumb: *When in doubt, throw it out.*

If you're not sure you should be making the decision to discard a particular item, ask your supervisor. The point is that you need to be

When in doubt, throw it out.

tough about not keeping superfluous items that can pile up, waste space, and become a distraction. Don't let such items sit on your desk, credenza, computer return, the top of your filing cabinet, or any other surface. Similarly, don't let them accumulate inside a drawer or cabinet.

And don't waste time about it. Rule Number 1 about processing paperwork is: Don't wait to make the decision. People often hang onto items they could throw away, or they don't make that decision until weeks or months later, when their workspace is in such a mess that they can't find papers and documents they need. Be proactive, and be consistent. Use the Trash terminal.

The Out-Tray

The Out-Tray is the only exception to the rule about having no physical trays in your workspace. You will want to use a tray to serve as this terminal. Keep your Out-Tray in a location where anyone who comes

> ## *FREQUENTLY ASKED QUESTION*
> ### Why do you make an exception to the "no trays" rule for the Out-Tray?
>
> There are a couple of reasons why it's useful to keep your outbound items in a real tray. The physical tray will hold your outbound papers and files so that they won't just be lying in a pile where they might get mixed up with other materials. In addition, the Out-Tray as a physical reality—the only "real" tray you have—serves as a reminder that what's in it needs to be dispersed promptly. You never want the Out-Tray to fill up; you would be prudent to empty its contents each time you leave your workspace, or have your assistant empty it every time he or she comes in.
>
> Thus we are allowing for the fact that a small number of items can and will accumulate in your Out-Tray—temporarily—until they are sent on their way. In contrast, your Virtual In-Tray should never be allowed to accumulate items. At all times while you are seated at your desk, your Virtual In-Tray must be clear for the next arriving piece of information.

to pick up items can find it readily, and where you yourself can easily place items for delivery. Figure 13 shows the ideal location for your Out-Tray, on the end of your credenza.

If you don't have a credenza

The guiding principles about where to keep your Out-Tray are that it be (a) outside your 180—the 180 degrees of your sight line from periphery to periphery as you sit facing your primary work area—and

(b) a place that makes it easy to empty when you're on the way out of your office or cubicle. For example, it can be on a bookshelf near the doorway, the end of a printer table, or the top of a file cabinet—as long as it sits where you see it on your way out, reminding you to empty it.

The Out-Tray has a very specific function: it momentarily holds items that belong outside the confines of your workspace. It doesn't matter what the item is or what stage of completion it's in; if its next destination is somewhere outside your office, it goes into your Out-Tray.

Every time you get up and leave your office—to go to a meeting, the coffee area, or the rest room; to go for lunch, or just to stretch your legs—you can easily take the Out-Tray contents with you and deliver them. This is a good habit to get into.

If you have an office assistant, ask this person to do the same thing every time they come into your office. To make all destinations clear, you can use Post-it notes or other "stickies," labeling each item or bundle according to its destination (for example, "Emma F.," "Warren," "HR," or "Mail pick-up").

That's all there is to learn about the Out-Tray terminal. It is as simple as it appears. Just remember to use your Out-Tray liberally, like your trash receptacle, and empty it often by moving items on to their next destination.

Your Paper File System

What do you think of when you think of files? If you're like most of us, you probably think of manila folders containing letters, reports, documents, and other paper-based information. You may also think of electronic (computer) files.

Let's concentrate for now on the physical terminal in your office called the File System. The File System, of course, includes the familiar paper files hanging in your filing cabinet. However, I want you to think of it as comprising a wider variety of materials: contact information, bulky items such as sections of large projects, and certain objects that do not fit inside a filing cabinet, for example, rolled-up charts and posters, or three-dimensional pieces such as architectural models.

As you can see, we are now talking about a terminal that may have more than one specific location within your workspace. Figure 13 shows three possible places that might all serve as parts of your File System: the filing drawer in your desk, a particular shelf in a bookcase, and the obvious place, your file cabinet.

File cabinet(s)

Perhaps you have more than one file cabinet. Both, or all of them, are components of your File System. Generally, you will want to use the cabinets for flat files within manila file folders, which in turn are kept within hanging folders (Pendaflex or another brand). You may want to reserve a particular drawer, for example the bottom drawer of a file cabinet, for bulky items such as book manuscripts or sets of architectural drawings that don't fit well in folders. We discussed the ideal scheme for organizing files by Client, Project, or Task during the purge process (Technique #1: see pages 17–37), and you might find it useful to return to that discussion as you continue to set up your File System.

Be sure to leave space within a file cabinet for your Library, as we also discussed in Technique #1 (see page 30). Mark it clearly, and reserve the space for newspaper clippings, trade journal articles, Web printouts, procedure sheets, and any other materials of a reference or instructional character that you want to be able to retrieve later.

Desk drawer

Another space that you will use as part of the File System is the filing drawer of your desk, which we mentioned in "The Purge." Your desk file drawer is the appropriate location for work files that you use frequently throughout the day, as well as files that are confidential. All files that you keep in this location should be only for your use.

Other files that belong in the desk filing drawer are those concerning personal matters that you can deal with only during business hours. Examples are files relating to your car or home insurance, home improvement or construction contracts, personal finance, and other personal or family matters—matters that require you to consult with your insurance agent, investment counselor, home contractor or plumber, medical personnel, or others whom you can contact only during working hours.

Objects that don't fit

What if you have objects that don't fit in your file cabinet or desk filing drawer, such as those charts, posters, or models we mentioned earlier? Look around your office, and the answer might be obvious. If you have a bookcase, you can reserve a particular shelf, or part of a shelf, that will serve the purpose. If you have a closet or vertical storage cabinet, there might be a handy shelf or two inside.

If you have an object that is attractive or a completed project worthy of showing off to visitors, put it on a shelf for display. A well-designed architectural model, for example, is something you should want clients to see. The same goes for a prize-winning ad page, a sample engine part that your team designed, a trophy or Lucite award plaque you earned for your performance, or indeed any product, report, or other artifact that you completed and now consider an object of pride. Just don't let your shelves get cluttered. Keep them looking presentable and professional.

> **If you have a completed project worthy of showing off, put it on a shelf for display.**

But what, exactly, distinguishes the materials that belong in your File System from those other terminals? The answer to this question keys in to the function of additional terminals—the Turtle, which we discussed in Technique #5, plus the Pending and Reading terminals (Techniques #10 and #12). Those terminals are for holding *work in progress*. The File System, in contrast, is primarily for storing *completed work*.

Note: As you will see in the discussion of the Pending terminal, there is a use for your filing cabinet related to work in progress, namely to serve as a "Home" for projects awaiting someone else's input. This will be clarified when we discuss Technique #10.

Think of your files as a *system of retrieval.* Your File System is not something static, so you should treat it as an active tool with an important purpose. You use it to store information for instant retrieval when you need it. And as you continue to build your File System, make sure you always keep a supply of everyday file-building materials close at hand—extra folders, labels, tabs, and whatever special pen or label marker you like to use.

Active files versus archival files

So far, we have been talking about *active files*—files on matters that are still relevant, even if the work has been completed. You probably also have files that you are never likely to need. Perhaps they contain data on a project your company completed years ago and it has been completely replaced or superseded by a new project. Perhaps you have files on a legal case that is closed and no longer requires any following-up. Or maybe you have files for a former client that has moved to Timbuktu and you never expect to hear from again; or an organization that no longer exists, a product line that has been retired, and so on. In short, the files pertain to fully completed work and have no value now or in the future. However, you believe the files *could* be needed at some future time for documentation purposes, governmental purposes, or legal reasons.

Any such files should be archived. If your organization has a central archive or off-site location, that's the best place for these files. If not, you will need to designate a space in your office for them. Some possibilities are the bottom drawer of a file cabinet, one end of a bookshelf, or a location in a closet. It is essential that you keep your archival files separated from your active files.

In summary

Your File System is a vital feature in your office that provides a logical and consistent method of storing and instantly retrieving materials pertaining to completed work. It is the only terminal that has multiple locations, which may include:

- One or more file cabinets holding conventional paper files organized by Client, Project, or Task, as well as certain bulky items such as manuscripts, and containing your Library of reference and instructional clippings and printouts

FREQUENTLY ASKED QUESTION
When should I move a file from the active area of my File System to the archives?

Generally, a file becomes archival material when it pertains to a project, case, or other matter that is no longer relevant in any active way. It is not likely to require follow-up by you or anybody else. You are not likely to refer to it for information at any time in the future. You do not need any data contained in the file—or if you do, the data are available somewhere else in your active files, on your organization's computer network, or in some other location readily accessible to you. You do not discard the file, however, because there is some possibility that it might be needed in the future for legal, governmental, or documentation purposes.

Files that remain active, on the other hand, are still relevant to current and future projects or cases. For example, a case is closed, but you might need to do some follow-up work for the client. That is an active file.

There are many possible gray areas. Let's say you've completed a project and no follow-up is needed, but the files contain documented procedures and lessons that may be applicable to current projects. It's up to you to decide whether to keep the files active or to archive them. As another example, your company has finalized a business venture, but the files contain data that might be useful in future deals. Active or archive? It's your call.

- The filing drawer of your desk, holding files that you use frequently, files that are confidential, and personal files
- One or more shelves of a bookcase for displaying completed projects or for holding items that don't fit inside a file cabinet
- Your archives, either a location within your workspace or a central archive maintained by your company

Having a functional, intuitive file system is extremely important to your working efficiency. If you closely follow the advice I've laid out, you will have a tremendously effective system for storing and instantly retrieving the records of your completed projects. This system will complement and mesh perfectly with your system for handling current project materials.

TECHNIQUE #10:
Pending
Develop a follow-up system as a whole new way of life

Like the Turtle, the Pending terminal holds work in progress. What's different about Pending, though, is that Pending items represent work on which you cannot go any further until something takes place over which you have no direct control: you need some crucial input from another person, or you must wait for a scheduled event to happen before you can finish the work.

Here's an example: you are writing a proposal for a product that requires parts that your company buys from a supplier, and your colleague, Lynne, is responsible for pricing those parts. You have completed the entire proposal except for factoring in the parts costs, but you haven't yet received the data you need from Lynne. This is an example of work you cannot complete until someone else gives you crucial input.

Now let's say that you're preparing a quarterly business report for your company. All the data is in and you have written the text, but you cannot officially finish the report and send it off for printing and distribution until the board of directors meets

> The Pending terminal holds work that you cannot complete until you get crucial input from someone else, or until some scheduled event takes place.

to certify the quarterly results. This is an example of work you cannot complete until a scheduled event takes place.

In both of these cases, you cannot go any further with the project until something happens that is beyond your direct control. Here's what you do now: Take the work that you've done, place it in your Pending terminal, and log it in your calendar or PDA on the follow-up date. (Technique #11 will be about using the calendar/PDA log in detail.)

The following comparison will help you tell the difference between items that belong in your Turtle and those that belong in Pending:

Turtle	Pending
Items that you *can* work on, but they are not as important as the project that is before you now	Items that you *cannot* work on, no matter how much available time you have, because you need input from someone else or because some scheduled event has to happen first

Location of Pending terminal

The ideal place for the Pending terminal is in the filing drawer of your desk, *in front of all other files in that drawer.* That will make it easy for you to retrieve the Pending files when you are ready to complete the project—that is, when you get the needed input or after the scheduled event takes place.

Place your Pending files in a hanging folder clearly labeled "Pending" to make sure they don't get mixed up with other files that you keep in the drawer.

Note: You use the Pending terminal for pending tasks that do not have an existing "home" elsewhere in your files. See the following discussion.

Pending files that already have a "Home"

If you already have a folder in your File System related to the task that's now pending, that is what I call the file's Home, and I recommend keeping the Pending material there instead of in your separate Pending area. For example, let's say you have an ongoing work relationship with the Acme Freight Company and you organize your File System by Client. In your filing cabinet you have a folder labeled "Acme Freight." It makes sense to keep your current Pending task together with these files. When you log the pending work in your scheduling calendar, you will assign the task the symbol Ⓗ to remind you that it is filed in its Home.

FREQUENTLY ASKED QUESTION

If all of my pending work is related to Clients, Projects, or Tasks for which I already have files, do I even need a separate Pending terminal?

In theory, no. If you have no "orphan" information—that is, none that is without a Home—your pending work items all get filed in their "Home" locations. However, you will undoubtedly work on activities someday for which you don't have an existing Client, Project, or Task folder in your File System. Therefore, it is essential to have a separate Pending terminal.

Pending Holding Area (PHA)

If you have Pending materials that are too bulky to fit in the appropriate filing drawer, create a Pending Holding Area (PHA), similar to your Turtle Holding Area (THA), and keep the bulky materials there until you are ready to work on them again. Make sure that this is a separate location from your THA; you don't want to mix up Turtle and Pending items. You do *not* need a Turtle Sheet for Pending materials, because you will be logging them in your calendar or PDA (Technique #11).

Pending materials held by your "admin" (P-A)

If you have an administrative assistant, or "admin," there may be times when your admin holds the materials for a pending task. I'll tell you in Technique #11 how to remind yourself where these materials are.

Pending files in your computer

Of course, you might have active work files in your computer (electronic files) that fit the definition of pending—you cannot complete the task until someone else gives you input or a scheduled event takes place. We'll discuss this situation in the next chapter. For now, let's focus on paper files and other physical materials that make up a pending task.

Other uses for Pending

Another good way to use the Pending terminal is to keep materials, ideas, or questions in it that are related to upcoming activities. For example, let's say you're meeting with Bob, Susan, and Jeremy a week from tomorrow. You've jotted down some specific questions to ask Jeremy, and you have some new graphics that Susan asked you to bring to the meeting. Put these in a separate file within your Pending folder, and you'll have them ready to go when the meeting time comes. To remind you of the questions and graphics, add the symbol Ⓟ to the entry for the meeting on your calendar or organizer.

Pending also works well for event tickets. If you have tickets for a concert, sports event, or play, for example, you might want to keep them in your Pending terminal. Any related information, such as driving directions or parking instructions, can be clipped or stapled to the tickets. Again, enter the Ⓟ symbol next to the date and time of the event. That way, you'll have everything you need when the date of the event arrives.

Pending work obviously requires follow-up, and that, in turn, means keeping track of a project's schedule. You will need to know how to use the Pending terminal in coordination with your calendar or PDA, the subject of the next Technique. But what you have learned in the preceding discussion will set you up to smoothly follow up work that cannot be completed immediately.

TECHNIQUE #11:
Personal Organization System
Set up your PDA or calendar book to coordinate your scheduling effectively

With our busy schedules, we all need a tool to keep track of our appointments, meetings, and events. You can turn your calendar or PDA into a Personal Organization System that not only handles these tasks but also coordinates with your Pending terminal to guarantee timely follow-through on work projects. Your Personal Organization System is another terminal, another tool, in your productivity toolkit.

I recommend that you use either a paper-based organizer, such as a calendar book, or an electronic organizer. The electronic organizer can be the calendar software on your computer, for example, or it can be on a handheld device (often called a personal digital assistant, or PDA) made by PalmOne, BlackBerry, Sony, Dell, or another company. It doesn't particularly matter what we call these—organizers, scheduling tools, or calendars—but you need to settle on one to serve as the center of your Personal Organization System.

During the purge (Technique #1), you got rid of all calendars but one and consolidated all-important information onto your primary calendar, either paper or digital. It is important that you do this. Having more than one functioning calendar or scheduling tool gives you too much opportunity to get important dates mixed up. You might schedule a meeting for Tuesday, the 20th at 10:30 a.m. on one calendar; then, looking at your other calendar some days later, you schedule an appointment with your eye doctor for the same time. Or here's a real nightmare: You have a performance review scheduled for, say, Thursday at 1:30 p.m. You've entered the appointment in your calendar book, which is on your desk. You go to an off-site sales meeting that morning, and your new client invites you to lunch afterward. You pull your PDA out of a pocket and check it. Nothing on it. You get back to the office at 2:15, and—oh, no, you've missed that crucial performance review.

See what I mean? Chaos lurks in wait for you every day when you operate with more than one scheduling tool.

The same rule holds for both your business and personal or family appointments: *Use only one scheduling tool.* Keep track of your personal and family events on the same calendar or electronic device that you use for your business appointments. You don't want to miss your son's piano recital because you aren't looking at your personal calendar when you schedule a late-afternoon meeting or a weekend office retreat. By the same token, you don't want to miss a dinner appointment with a client because you're looking at your personal calendar, which has a tennis match scheduled for the same time.

Log your phone messages

Use your Personal Organization System for logging phone messages when you need to return a call at a specific time. Enter them on your calendar as if they were appointments. That way, you won't get into situations where you have to choose between ducking out of a meeting to make the call and missing the party who's expecting to hear from you.

Use the Personal Organization System to schedule incoming calls also. If a client who is impossible to reach agrees to call you on her cell phone between 5:00 and 5:15 p.m. on Thursday, you want to make sure you will be available at that time. You need to have that telephone appointment staring out at you from your scheduling tool.

Where to Locate Your Personal Organization Terminal

If you use a paper-based organizer, such as a calendar book, it should be large enough to hold all the information you need to keep in it, but small enough to sit at the top of your desk, as shown in Figure 14. I recommend the size that holds 5½" by 8½" sheets. Your organizer should be in clear view at all times, and always open to the current day.

If you use a handheld electronic device, you should keep it out on your desk while you are in your workspace. I recommend placing it in the same position where the appointments calendar is located in Figure 14.

Take it with you

Imagine that I'm a client of yours. We've been having lunch together in a restaurant. We've had a fruitful conversation, and as we are about to end our meeting, I say to you, "Can we meet again on Friday at 11 a.m.?"

What, exactly, do you do or say at this moment?

Often I ask this question during my seminars. One time, Sam answered, "Good idea, but my calendar is in my office. I'll have to get back to you." Cory said, "I take my PDA with me, and if it says I'm free then, I schedule the meeting. If not, we negotiate a time." Kristin said she carried her pocket organizer with her in her briefcase and always checked it before making a commitment. Cory and Kristin are on the ball. Sam, however, is like most of the people I meet with, especially those who are executives or managers. They have to call me back. Will they remember to? Are they writing a note to themselves on a cocktail napkin? Must I bother them with a phone call tomorrow, and will I be able to reach them?

Figure 14

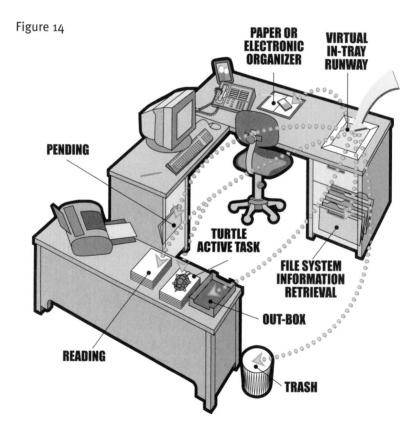

In this day and age, there is no excuse for Sam. His inability to make an appointment on the spot is not only obsolete, it is unprofessional. He should not make clients, business partners, customers, vendors, or anybody else have to wait for him to call them back.

This is why you need to have your scheduling tool with you at all times. Take it with you when you attend meetings and other events during which you might need to check your schedule. You never know when you'll need to make an appointment, so you must assume you will always need to.

If it's your admin's responsibility

What if someone else handles your schedule—your administrative assistant or secretary, for example?

In that case, you should always be prepared to check in with that person. Carry a cellular phone and call your admin to schedule the meeting on the spot. Don't keep the other party waiting.

The PC/PDA connection

Many PDAs and other handheld devices contain a calendar that can be "docked" with your desktop computer. Used in tandem, your computer calendar and the dockable handheld device work as if they were one calendar system.

The docking feature enables you to easily synchronize the data on your handheld device with the calendar software on your computer (for example, Microsoft Outlook). If you are comfortable using them both, by all means, do—just make sure you *synchronize the two calendars at the beginning of every workday, and again at the end of the workday.* Follow the instructions that come with the product. Do not forget to synchronize your calendar devices, or you risk chaos in

> You may use the calendar feature of a dockable handheld device together with your desktop computer if you synchronize them at the beginning and end of every workday.

your scheduling just as if you were using two calendars.

The same holds true if your PDA is capable of a wireless connection to the scheduling software on your desktop computer. Today's handheld computing devices are little miracles of technology with many exciting uses. However you use yours, the important aspect from the perspective of your Personal Organization System is to manage your schedule from one—and only one—system.

Using Your Personal Organization System with Pending

Because all of your Pending information is, by definition, incomplete, you need a mechanism for tracking due dates and follow-ups. Let's return now to the example we mentioned while discussing Technique #10. You're waiting to finish a proposal until your colleague, Lynne, gets back to you with information about parts costs. Now you call Lynne to request the necessary information.

It is very important that you ask her to commit to a specific date. For example, you might say, "Lynne, when may I expect you to get back to me about this?" and she replies, "Next Monday." As soon as you get off the phone, go directly to your calendar or PDA. For next Monday, enter a note to remind you that day to call Lynne again for the cost information: for example, "Lynne—parts costs." To remind yourself where to find the proposal that this pertains to, write one of the following symbols in the left margin of your calendar directly beside the note to call Lynne:

Use this symbol	If the proposal is
Ⓟ	In your Pending terminal
ⓅHA	In your Pending Holding Area
Ⓗ	The proposal's home file
ⒺP ⒺH	In your electronic files (i.e., on your computer)
Ⓟ-A	Being held by your administrative assistant

Note: "EP" stands for electronic Pending, and "EH" for electronic Home. EP and EH are file locations on your computer rather than in your paper system.

Now you have a solid reminder to call Lynne for the information you need to finish the report. On Monday, you will see the reminder and the symbol, and you won't have to stop and think about where the report is.

You can use a similar trick for keeping track of the event tickets we mentioned on page 104. Enter the event—a basketball game, opera, garden show, and so on—in your Personal Organization System (calendar book, organizer, or electronic scheduling tool); put the tickets in the Pending terminal, and add the Ⓟ symbol to the entry in your organizer.

Here's one more example. Suppose you are an accountant, and one of your longstanding clients is Jespersen Realty. You were working on

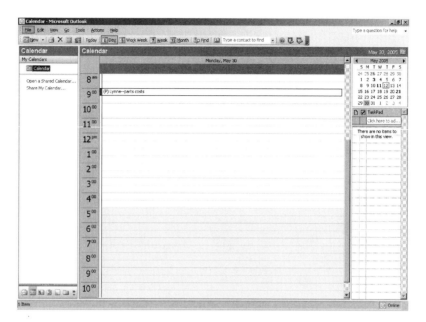

Figure 15

a financial statement for Jespersen last week when you discovered you couldn't go any further until you got budget projections from your colleague Tom. You placed the Jespersen materials in their Home, the existing file folder where you keep all records for Jespersen. You marked on your scheduling calendar "Tom—Jespersen projections" on the page for next Monday, and you added to your calendar the symbol Ⓗ to remind you where the file is.

In the Introduction to this book, we talked about the *pleasure to forget*. By using your Pending terminal and Personal Organization System together as I've just taught you, you can relax and forget about the details of your incomplete report until the time arrives for getting back to it. There's no way that important information will fall through the cracks and get lost.

Personal Organization System: Summary

To make your Personal Organization System work, you make calendar appointments to track anything that happens at a scheduled time—a business meeting, interview, lunch date, family birthday party, and indeed all sorts of events that are important to you. You also make calendar appointments for phone calls that must occur at a specific time, whether it is a proactive call, a return call, or a call that you are expecting from someone else.

Keep in mind that we are working with a *single scheduling system.* The dinner party you will attend Saturday evening and your daughter's basketball game on Sunday are logged in the same organizer as the briefing with your assistant next Monday, your meeting with your accountant on Tuesday, and your dental check-up on Thursday. One brain, one organizer—business and personal.

TECHNIQUE #12:
Reading
Organize, prioritize, and get through all of your reading

If you're like most of us, you need to do a lot of reading in your work: reports, letters, procedural manuals, business journals, email attachments, informational web pages, and more. You can't read every article and instruction sheet immediately as they come across your desk, and they can pile up quickly. Some of us may develop a sense of guilt watching those materials accumulate. "I should be doing my reading," we might think. "Look at all those magazines and journals on my desk."

There's a better way. You can effectively cull your reading materials, set the essential ones aside for reading at a convenient time, and escape those feelings of being overwhelmed by the stack. The method is similar to how you handle tasks in the Turtle (Technique #5). However, you don't want to put the reading materials in your Turtle stack, because you need to reserve that for active work projects. Where do you put your items for reading?

In the Reading terminal. Next to your Turtle, you create an orderly stack of materials that will serve as your Reading terminal. (See Figure 10 on page 65 for the ideal location.) This is where you will hold items you need to read until you can get to them.

For handling articles, here's the procedure I recommend: As soon as you receive a magazine, journal, or other periodical—and I mean *immediately,* not ten minutes later—open it to the table of contents (TOC). Quickly scan the TOC and ask yourself two questions:

- Is there anything in this TOC that is important to me now?
- Is there anything that could be important to me in the future?

If your answer to either question is yes, clip out or copy the article pages and staple them together. (Clip them out if the source is a magazine or other publication that is yours to keep; copy them if you intend to pass the publication on to someone else.)

FREQUENTLY ASKED QUESTION
Why do I have to clip or copy the articles? Why can't I just put the journals in the Reading stack and bookmark the pages?

There's a simple psychological reason for clipping or copying the articles. The stack of reading materials will be much thinner, much less daunting, if you keep just the relevant article pages there.

There's also an issue of concentration. With just the articles you need, you won't be distracted by ads or tempted to read other articles that aren't of importance to you. You will stay focused on what you need to read, and you will get through it much faster. You'll no longer have that growing pile of reading materials.

Note: It is better to staple the pages together rather than use a paper clip. Paper clips can easily fall off a bundle of sheets, and sometimes they will attach themselves to other, adjacent pages. If you don't like stapling the sheets, another alternative is to use binder clips.

If an article is important to you now, it goes to your Reading terminal. If it's an item for possible future reading, put it in your Library, which you set up during your office purge.

As you do with the Turtle, stack the readings in order of priority, with the most important or most immediate readings on top.

Be proactive

You probably know how easy it is to leave your reading time to chance. I strongly recommend that you be proactive about this and schedule time that you can dedicate solely to reading. For example, you might plan to arrive at work ninety minutes early two mornings each week and use that extra time to catch up on your reading. In addition, you might want to grab one or two articles off the top of the stack as you head for lunch. I definitely urge you *not* to take your reading home with you. Remember that you are changing your work habits to have more quality time for yourself and your family. Taking your work reading home will sabotage that important goal.

Another Turtle trick is useful for the Reading terminal: large or bulky items, such as a chapter that you cannot tear out of a thick book or a report contained in an oversized binder, can be held elsewhere and represented in your prioritized Reading stack by a Turtle Sheet. You don't need to fill out this Turtle Sheet quite as much; just give the title of the reading piece and add its location ("Top shelf of bookcase," "Bottom shelf of vertical cabinet," or wherever you're putting it). If the title doesn't describe the contents sufficiently, you can also add a brief note, for example, "Article on effective sales techniques" or "Review of new enterprise software." If you need to read something by a specific date, add that information to the Completion Date field. (For information on creating Turtle Sheets, see pages 68–73.)

Stack your readings in order of priority, and use the equivalent of Turtle Sheets for large or bulky items.

Like your Turtle and Outbox, you'll want to keep your Reading terminal prioritized and contained. Do not let your Reading terminal overlap with your Turtle terminal, and do not let the stack grow so high that you worry about being unable to get through your reading. A slim, orderly Reading terminal helps keep your mind free from anxiety and stress.

Take my advice: get your reading materials under control, make time to read them—*regularly*—and discover how easy it is to stay on top of the literature that is relevant to your work.

Mastering Your Tools of Electronic Communication

Email and voice-mail: Twenty years ago, these two terms would have made us stop in our tracks and say, "What in the world are you talking about?"

Laptop computers, personal digital assistants, cellular phones; hand-held devices as small as our wallet that combine the functions of a computer, a telephone, a calendar and schedule monitor, a music player, a video screen, and—hey, Mom, look this way!—a camera! Today all of these tools are integral features of our working lives, and our personal lives as well. We couldn't live without them.

But sometimes they drive us crazy. How do we keep up with all the information? How do we coordinate what we do in the office and what we do on the road?

In this day and age, mastering your tools of electronic communication is paramount to achieving your maximum productivity. This section of the book offers the best advice I can give you for organizing your electronic information and keeping it organized at peak efficiency.

Don't be a slave to electronics—make them your slave. That's what they're for.

TECHNIQUE #13:
Email
Go home with ZERO messages in your In-box at the end of every day

Of all the Black Holes of information we mentioned earlier—trays and standing file folders, multiple calendars, and so on—the single biggest Black Hole is your email In-box. This is the dreaded place where information can get hopelessly lost amid dozens, if not hundreds, of incoming messages. I know people who have accumulated thousands of messages in their In-box and have practically no hope of catching up. This doesn't need to happen.

Let's start with a simple principle: *email is no different from any other type of information that comes your way.* There is nothing magical or threatening about an email message. It doesn't matter if it's a request for information, a body of crucial data for an active task, an invitation to a conference, or simply a reminder of an upcoming event—*you treat it all the same way.*

How can that be possible? By thinking of your In-box as your electronic Vin-Tray and using it accordingly.

Virtual In-Tray, Electronic Version

Remember the email folders you created in your computer system during the purge? You should have them available now, and they should have the following labels: Archive, Clients (or Projects or Tasks, depending on how you've set up your paper filing system), Library/Reference, Pending (EP), Personal, Reading, and Turtle (ET).

I think you can see where this is leading. You treat your email In-box just like the Virtual In-Tray on your desk. Email messages land in your In-box. You read them, one at a time, and make a judgment: This one goes into the Clients folder because it's information requiring no work. That one goes to Pending because I'm awaiting further information (and I instantly log the follow-up date on my paper or electronic calendar). Here's one containing a lengthy article on Internet sales techniques; I'll want to

Your email In-box is your electronic Vin-Tray.

Figure 16

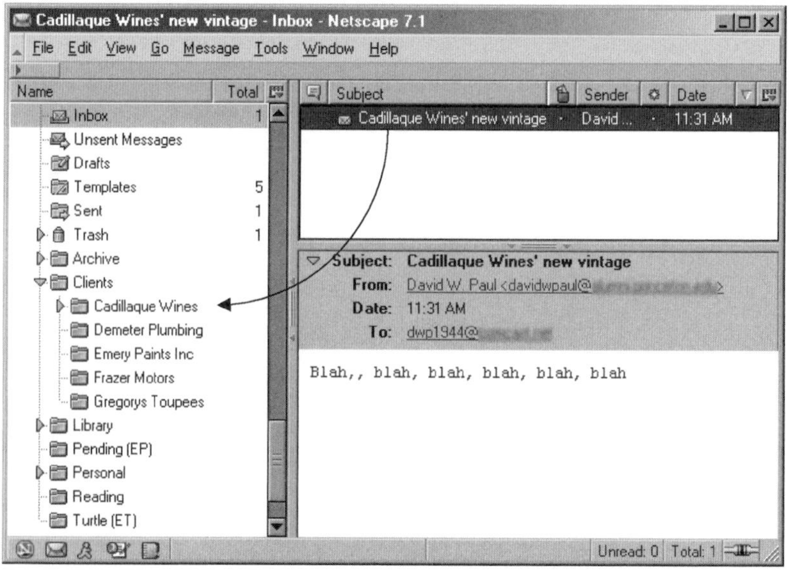

read that soon, so it goes to my Reading folder. Here's a message from my cousin Tess; that goes into the Personal folder.

Get the picture? For the most part, you're dealing with electronic folders whose functions are parallel to the physical terminals described in previous techniques:

- **Pending (EP)** and **Reading** mean exactly what they do for your paper items; the "EP" after Pending stands for "electronic pending," an abbreviation that will be used as a locator in your Personal Organization System.

- **Turtle (ET)** corresponds in function to the Turtle containing your active-task paper items; "ET" stands for "Electronic Turtle." See page 130 for information on how to coordinate your electronic Turtle with your physical (paper) Turtle.

- **Library/Reference** is similar to the Library you created within your physical File Cabinet. Here is where you put email messages containing specific information and articles that you might want for future retrieval. (See page 30.)

- The Personal folder is where you hold personal messages, much as you hold your personal paper files in your desk drawer. (See page 32.)

- **Clients**, **Projects**, or **Tasks** is where you hold (a) electronic files pertaining to completed tasks and (b) pending tasks that have a "Home" among these files. (For the meaning of "Home," see page 101.) Name this folder *Client* if you file your paper records by client; name it *Projects* if you file them by project, and *Tasks* if you file them by task.

Your electronic folders parallel the physical terminals you set up earlier.

You already set up the folder system for handling email during the purge. You should also have cleared out your unused email folders and transferred all of your messages to the new electronic "terminals." You also cleared out your In-box during the purge, but you may have new messages since you set up the electronic terminals. Check it again now and transfer all messages to the appropriate electronic terminals.

Note: If you can make the decision about where to transfer a message by reading only the heading in your In-box, great. If you need to open the message, read just enough of it to "taxi" it to the appropriate electronic terminal.

Delete any unused email folders that you yourself created as soon as you're sure they are no longer needed.

Now start dealing directly with messages as they reach your In-box. Deal with them promptly, and there should never again be a backlog.

Email Folders = Electronic Terminals

The following paragraphs will give you specific pointers on how to use your email folders as electronic terminals.

Reading

The Reading folder works just like your paper-based Reading stack. (See Technique #12.) Any information you get that you don't have time to read immediately goes here. As an alternative, you can print out the email and put it in the paper-based Reading terminal (the stack next to your Turtle).

Note: If you store the information electronically, it's important to print the first page of each item and place it in your (paper) Reading stack so that you have a physical representation of it.

Web pages for Reading

Many of us frequently come across web sites containing articles that are timely and relevant to our work, but we simply cannot read them immediately. You need to save them in a place where you have instant access when you're ready to read them. There are two possible ways to do this:

- Print the web pages, staple them together, and add them to your paper Reading terminal;

OR

- Save a link to the pages in your Reading email folder. With the first Web page open, choose *File > Save As* (in Netscape, this command is *File > Save Page As*), click through your folder locations to your Reading folder, and save the page there. When you are ready to read the files, you can open them by clicking the saved link within your Reading folder.

> Print out or "Save As" useful web pages and have them available when you're ready to read them.

Note: If you choose the second option, keeping the web pages in your computer, it is essential that you print the first page of each article and place it in your (paper) Reading stack as a reminder of the article in its electronic form. If the article is only one, two, or three pages long, you might find it simpler to print it entirely. Staple the pages together, and keep them in your paper Reading terminal.

Once you've done this, you will never have to ask yourself, "Now where did I see that interesting piece about the latest widget technology?" You will know the article is either in your Reading stack or accessible by Internet link within your electronic Reading folder, and you can read it during the time you allocate for reading.

The procedure you use for managing web page reading applies to all forms of materials that you hold electronically for future reading. That would include files sent to you as email attachments, as well as documents that you download from your company's network.

Turtle (ET)

You use this folder, the electronic equivalent of your paper Turtle, to store active-task materials that you receive in electronic form (email messages or files). (For information on the Turtle, see Technique #5.)

Whenever you receive an email message relating to an active task that requires more than a moment to complete, drag and drop it into the Turtle (ET) folder. Immediately do one of the following:

- Print out the first sheet, and place that in your physical Turtle—the one holding your paper tasks—according to its priority in the stack. Mark the top left corner with the ⒺⓉ symbol.

or

• Create a Turtle Sheet for the email message (on paper!) and put that in your physical Turtle according to its priority in the stack. Be sure to give the task a clear, distinctive title on the Turtle Sheet and write "ET" in the Location of Information Needed field. (For information on creating Turtle Sheets, see pages 68–73.)

Now you have something in your Turtle stack to represent the active task that resides in your computer. This is very important, because the goal is to have one single place for keeping all of your active tasks—all the work you have to do that is not as important or immediate as the task you are currently working on.

Note: If the original task document is three pages long or less, an alternative to keeping in your ET is to can print it out and place it in your Turtle stack along with your other active tasks. If you do this, you don't need a Turtle Sheet. You can either delete the original email or electronic file containing the task, or file it in your electronic Clients, Projects, or Tasks folder.

Pending

The electronic Pending folder works like the Pending terminal in your desk drawer and file cabinet. (See Technique #10.) This folder is for email messages or computer files containing active tasks on which you cannot proceed until you receive information or input from someone else (or until a specific date or deadline occurs). When you drag and drop an item into the electronic Pending folder, immediately note the item on your Personal Organization System and add an (EP) symbol in the left margin of your calendar notation.

Getting the Most Out of Your Handheld Device

For many of us, the advent of handheld computing devices, called personal digital assistants (PDAs), heralded something radically new in the way we keep track of our affairs—not only our work, but also the numerous happenings in our family and personal lives. With PDAs now married to the cell phone, wireless Internet connections have made it a *ménage à trois*; the addition of a music player and a digital camera has created a tool that is hard to describe in a short phrase. Whatever we call them, these pocket-sized instruments are a miracle of miniaturized electronics. If we learn their many features, they will support us in taking care of tasks we used to think we could not handle from any one location—let alone a *moving* location.

You don't need a PDA to make my organizing system work for you, but if you have a PDA, I encourage you to use it to its full advantage.

If you have one of these little wonders, I encourage you to make full use of its features. Concentrate on those functions that will make your life more efficient—the electronic calendar that you can synch up with your desktop computer calendar, for example, and the telephone book feature that will enable you to make contact while you are stuck in traffic en route to an important meeting.

However, you don't have to use all of the PDA's wonderful features to make my organizing system work for you. That should be particularly good news if, for whatever reason, you are holding off on obtaining a PDA and still using a paper-based organizer.

TECHNIQUE #14:
Voice-mail
Get all of your phone messages under control

If you implemented the last part of Technique #4, "Computer and Voice-mail Purge," you have already prepared your voice-mail system for effective use. Now I'm going to share with you some of my secrets for managing phone messages on an ongoing basis and making sure that you follow up every important call.

Voice-mail: Love It, Hate It

Voice-mail is a great tool that collects telephone messages when we can't take a call for whatever reason. Voice-mail has made those pesky little "While you were out" slips obsolete (for those of us who remember them). Voice-mail guarantees that our phone messages never get lost amid papers on our desk or incoming mail. What's not to like about it?

The backlog. The obligatory callbacks. People you'd rather not talk to. The temptation to put off dealing with messages until tomorrow or next week. The all-consuming telephone chaos. That's what's not to like.

Who do I have to call first? Where did I put that number? I really don't want to call Sherry; she's a good business contact, but she wants to sell me something that I don't think we need. I'll just pretend I never got her voice-mail. And then there's that message from my nephew Brad, wanting money for whatever reason.

132 The Instant Productivity Toolkit

If any of that sounds familiar, you should recognize it as a problem getting in the way of your working efficiency. Recall the approach I spelled out in Technique #4:

1. Copy down in a spiral-bound notebook the name and number of each caller, along with the essence of each call. You might also add the time of the call.
2. Delete each message from your voice-mail system as soon as you have collected the necessary information. Delete calls you do not have to return.
3. Prioritize your return calls.
4. Return the calls.

Proactive and Reactive Calls

A proactive phone call is one that you initiate; it's your idea, not somebody else's, and you dial the number. A reactive call is (a) when somebody calls you and you answer, or (b) a call you make in response to a voice-mail message. Proactive calls and case (a) reactive calls need no discussion; you know how to handle them. Case (b) reactive calls—those to people who have left voice-mail and expect you to call back—deserve some attention here. If you do not have an efficient system for managing your callbacks, you can quickly lose control of them.

Use the spiral-bound notebook

Let's return to the spiral-bound notebook I asked you to use for logging telephone messages. (See page 60.) You might be wondering why, in this gadget-filled electronic age, I recommend such old-fashioned "technology."

There are several reasons. In the first place, voice-mail is potentially one of the Black Holes of information. Phone messages can sit there, out of sight and out of mind, while your voice-mailbox fills up. In the meantime, there is no visible reminder that you have calls to answer. In particular, you have no incentive for answering those

> **Your notebook gives you a paper trail of phone messages you've returned — or not returned.**

calls you really don't want to deal with (yet know, in the back of your mind, that you need to). You're caught between *not remembering*, on the one hand, and a nagging sense of unfinished business on the other. The notebook is a visible reminder that getting your work done requires follow-up and follow-through.

Second, if you have both a desk phone and a cell phone—and most of us do—you will accumulate voice-mail in two different places. You absolutely need the notebook for consolidating your phone messages and prioritizing them.

A third reason is that your notebook provides a great paper trail. Writing your phone messages down in the notebook gives you a tangible record of calls you've received and calls you've returned.

Here's an example of why this is important: Suppose you have a vendor named Brian who left a message on the third of the month. You've tried several times to return his call, and when the two of you finally connect he complains that you haven't gotten back in touch with him. You can pull out your notebook and say, "Excuse me, Brian, but my records tell me I called you on the fourth, the seventh, and the tenth and left a message each time."

Keep that notebook next to your telephone, and take it with you when you leave the office with your cell phone.

FREQUENTLY ASKED QUESTION

I like to handle my voice-mail messages while driving, because that's time I don't spend doing anything else constructive. Don't you think that's a good idea?

Not a good idea. It's hard to remember somebody's phone number if you're concentrating on your driving—as you should be. And *don't even think about writing down messages and numbers while you're in the rush-hour traffic*—or at any other time of the day. Too many people cause accidents because they're dealing with non-driving matters.

To handle your voice-mail messages, you need to be in a place where you can log them, free of distraction and safe from the traffic. If you insist on doing this from your car, pull off the road first. Better yet, wait and do it in your office.

Note: Holding a cell phone in your hand while driving puts you and others in jeopardy. In fact, it is illegal in some parts of the United States. You'd be well advised to invest the few dollars it costs to purchase a headpiece that keeps your hands free.

Use shorthand codes

I use codes in my voice-mail notebook for keeping track of messages and follow-ups, and I recommend that you do likewise. I can jot the codes quickly near the beginning of each message, using a felt-tip pen in a color that jumps out from the sheet, like green or red. Here are the codes I use. Think of these as a kind of shorthand for common-sense instructions you give yourself about handling your voice-mail.

Code	Meaning
LM	<u>L</u>eft <u>M</u>essage (I left a message and am waiting for a call back)
AMTCB _____	<u>A</u>sked <u>M</u>e <u>T</u>o <u>C</u>all <u>B</u>ack on _____ (specific date)
(Tell ____)	Someone else who needs to know about the results of this call
(Underline)	Highlights of this conversation
T	<u>T</u>ransferred to next appropriate day (because it's incomplete)
✔	Completed

Returning calls: worst first

Here's a rule about returning calls that I find helpful: do the worst first. That is, start with those messages from people you don't like talking to. If you've got a message from someone who drives you crazy, put that person at the top of your list for callbacks.

I realize this advice may strike you as peculiar, if not downright weird, but here is my reasoning: if you postpone that call and start with people you prefer talking to, the person you don't want to talk to will be banging away in the back of your head. If Mr.

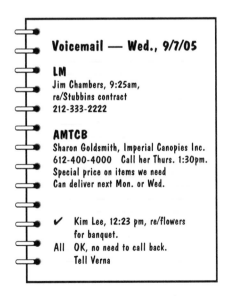

> **Voicemail — Wed., 9/7/05**
>
> **LM**
> Jim Chambers, 9:25am,
> re/Stubbins contract
> 212-333-2222
>
> **AMTCB**
> Sharon Goldsmith, Imperial Canopies Inc.
> 612-400-4000   Call her Thurs. 1:30pm.
> Special price on items we need
> Can deliver next Mon. or Wed.
>
> ✔   Kim Lee, 12:23 pm, re/flowers
>   for banquet.
> All OK, no need to call back.
>   Tell Verna

Figure 17

X is that person, and you first call Sally and Bob and Fred and Anna, you're going to hear a little voice saying, "Mr. X, Mr. X, Mr. X." So get that call out of the way. And if there are more on your list whom you also don't want to call, phone them next. This may seem like a bitter pill, but just watch yourself growing calmer once you've gotten the most difficult folks out of the way and started talking to those with whom you'd rather deal.

Don't lose track of any callbacks

If you get a lot of voice-mail, you will fill up pages quickly. As you flip through your notebook, you need to be careful about keeping track of which calls you have returned and, especially, which ones you haven't.

Here's what I do: I place a paper clip on a page when I've completed all callbacks on that page. If any page does not have a clip on it, I know there's at least one call on it that I need to return. I clip together multiple pages containing notes on calls I've returned. For multiple pages, a binder clip (as opposed to an ordinary paper clip) works best. *I do not clip a sheet if I haven't achieved resolution on a particular call.* If I have returned somebody's call but had to leave my own voice-mail message, I consider that an unresolved call and I do not clip the sheet it's on.

> **Clip pages together when you've completed all callbacks on those pages.**

At the end of each day, I turn to a fresh notebook sheet and copy onto it the relevant information from all calls I haven't returned and resolved.

Note: You may immediately see that, if you have many such calls at the end of a day, copying all the needed information can be a pain. That should serve as an incentive to take care of those calls promptly.

Keeping Up with Your Voice-mail, Always

If you use the tools I've described in the previous pages, you can get control of your voice-mail. Never again will you miss making an important return call, and you will have a record on paper of the results of all your callbacks. Thousands of my clients have succeeded with this technique. You can do it, too.

TECHNIQUE #15:
The Paper/PC Connection
Establish uniformity in your workflow system

One of the most important criteria for an efficient filing system is *uniformity*. If the conventions you use for your paper filing system differ from those of your computer files, anything from confusion to chaos will inevitably result. However, if your paper and computer files are consistent—if you organize them using the same conventions, and if the category and folder names are consistent—the flow of information within your organizing system will amaze you.

The same principle applies to all of the terminals we've been discussing in this book: all of the physical workspace tools, computer files, and email folders described in earlier pages. Uniformity and consistency within your physical and electronic systems will make your life easy. Storing and retrieving documents, finding email messages, following up on tasks and projects, and always staying on schedule will become embedded, so to speak, in your working habits.

Uniformity and consistency between paper and electronic systems will do wonders for your information flow.

The Paper/PC Connection is what I call my system for building uniformity into your workspace. All paper and electronic (computer) files pertaining to any specific work task or project are treated the same. The methods of processing information are consistent whether paper or electronic files are involved. Both the procedures and the terminology—the "language," if you will—are consistent. There is a Turtle and an electronic Turtle, a physical Library and an electronic Library/Reference, a paper Pending system and an electronic Pending folder, and so on. If you've applied my techniques so far, you, too, now have the same tools that I use to process my workflow.

Trash and Out-Tray have close counterparts in your electronic system, as in mine. When you delete a computer file or an email message, you are trashing it. Your computer has electronic containers for your trashed files: the Recycle Bin in Microsoft Windows systems and the Trash in Macintosh systems are the counterparts to your office wastebasket. The Trash folder in your email application plays the same role for unwanted email messages. The electronic equivalent of your Out-Tray is the Send function of your email software. The Send button, or its keyboard shortcut (typically CTRL+ S in the Windows system) is in fact more efficient than your physical Out-Tray because, obviously, you don't have to carry email messages or files to another person—you deliver them with a click of your mouse or two rapid finger motions on the keyboard.

Appointments, voice-mail, and the Paper/PC Connection

What we have already said about using your Personal Organization System—paper-based organizer, scheduling software, or PDA— assists you in making the Paper/PC Connection. When you annotate your calendar with the Ⓟ, Ⓗ, ⒺⓅ, ⒺⒽ, ⒺⓉ, or ⓅⒽⒶ symbols, you are creating a cross-reference that cuts across your paper and electronic systems.

The annotation symbols extend the Paper/PC Connection to your telephone. Yes, I know your telephone isn't your PC, but many people today have computer-based voice-mail and fax service, and some still make their email connection over a telephone line. So we are not stretching the language much by including our old friend the telephone in the Paper/PC Connection.

The point is that a truly efficient workflow is one that builds a high degree of uniformity and consistency into the way you handle electronic and paper-based materials. If you have set up your workflow system according to the fourteen techniques spelled out in the preceding chapters, you will have the foundations for managing your workflow in a way that guarantees your maximum productivity.

The next technique will take you on the road, away from your office, for a proven, effective approach to mobile working.

TECHNIQUE #16:
Mobility
Stay proactive and in control
while on the road

For millions of people today, work involves travel. It's common-place for office workers, managers, and executives to take their laptop and PDA on the road, along with their traditional, low-tech business necessities—briefcases, business cards, pens and pencils. More and more often, people ask me in my seminars what to do about their workflow system when they fly off to Houston, Detroit, Portland, Hartford, or wherever their job assignment takes them. They know they will spend some time on an airplane and in a hotel room; they intend to use that time productively, and they want to synchronize their on-the-road working system with the methods and tools I've taught them to use in their office.

You obviously can't take your office with you; with a small amount of planning, however, you can prepare your business trips for maximum productivity and workflow integration. Let's look at a technique that will support you as you take your business to other cities, whether distant or not so far away.

Mobile Turtle

First, you will want to make sure that you take care of your most important active tasks while traveling. These are in your Turtle, and so you need to make your Turtle "mobile." This does not mean picking up your entire Turtle stack, let alone what is in your Turtle Holding Area (THA), and loading it all into your briefcase. Rather, as you are getting ready for a particular trip, take a few minutes to do the following:

1. Determine the length of your trip (number of days, including travel time).
2. Estimate your focus time while traveling. This means the usable amount of time you will be in flight (or on a train, if that is how you're traveling). For example, if you're flying from Phoenix to Chicago, you might have three and a half hours each way, totaling seven hours.
3. Estimate your available down time while away, for example three nights with two usable hours each night, totaling six.
4. Add the hours you came up with in steps 2 and 3. In the example given, that would be thirteen hours.
5. Take with you that number of hours' worth of prioritized work from your paper Turtle, which will indicate what you'll need from your THA, and/or your electronic Turtle (ET).
6. Take along any ancillary information you need to complete the work, for example reference materials, relevant articles, and Client files.

Mobile Pending

To take care of Pending terminal requiring follow-up work that will come due while you're traveling, do the following:

1. Determine the time frame of your trip (exactly which dates you will be gone).
2. Add some time to your return date to cover any unexpected extension of your stay; for example, add an extra day or two. This

is important contingency planning, in case you don't get back to your office on schedule and there are Pending items that come due during that extended period.

3. Review your Personal Organization System for all Pending tasks coming due within this extended time frame.

4. Take with you all Pending items you've identified in step 3. The symbols in your Personal Organization System will indicate the location of those materials, for example your paper Pending Ⓟ, electronic Pending ⒺⓅ, and Pending Holding Area ⓅⒽⒶ.

5. Take also any ancillary information you need to complete the Pending work, like reference materials, relevant articles, and Client files.

Reading

Travel time is a great time to catch up on your business reading, so take along some items from your Reading stack.

Supplies

To facilitate keeping the work items in order while you travel, be sure to take along the following supplies:

- A folder containing blank Turtle Sheets
- A folder to hold your traveling Turtle
- A folder for your traveling Pending

These items will prepare you for staying in synch with your office terminals, keeping up with your work, and knowing that you have every project and task under control. You will take the *pleasure to forget* on the road with you.

Mental and Procedural Tools

Underlying much of the discussion in this book is the idea that high personal productivity depends on efficient working habits and sound procedures for carrying out the tasks assigned to us. The following four techniques bring this assumption front and center, describing some mental and procedural tools that I have found indispensable to success on the job. I always try to pass them on to clients who attend my seminars and training programs, and now I offer them to you. Mastering these uncomplicated techniques will give your productivity a further boost.

TECHNIQUE #17:
Finding What You Need
Name your files for instant retrieval

I'm sure you've had the experience, at least once and probably many times, of not being able to find a particular file in your computer. You knew it was there; you knew it had some specific information that you needed, but you couldn't remember the exact name of the file. It took you precious minutes, and maybe a long time, to find the file. Perhaps you never found it, or you found it only after you had to redo some research or went, tail between your legs, back to the person who had given you the information in the first place and asked for it again. I am going to teach you a simple trick that I guarantee will help you choose filenames you will remember.

The most common reason we "lose" a file in our computer system is that we don't give it the proper name—a name that is both intuitive and specific. And the most common reason behind this dilemma is that we name the file in a rush. We finish writing a document, designing a graphic, filling out a spreadsheet, whatever...and we want to move on to the next task. So we quickly assign a name to the file, save it, and close it.

When you name a file in a rush, the chances are very high that you will not be able to instantly retrieve that file later, because you didn't think it through. I urge you to *pause for five to ten seconds and think about the filename.* Chances are you'll come up with a new filename that is far easier to recall. I promise you that if you take just five to ten seconds, you will think of a filename that will enable you to retrieve it instantly a year later.

What is true for naming electronic files is just as true for naming paper files. Think about the name you're about to give that file. Give it that same five to ten seconds to make sure the filename is one you will always remember. Make the name as specific as necessary in order to associate it with the information you will need at a later time.

Not long ago, I was working with a man who had received some important information and wanted to create a file for it. When I asked him what it was, he said, "It's about the building that we're in." The building was the Wolfe Building, and so he wanted to name the file "Wolfe Building." I asked him then what the information was specifically about and he replied, "The fire code system." I asked him to stop and think whether "Wolfe Building" was a filename he would recall months later. I waited a few seconds in silence, and then he yelled out, "Fire Security."

> Don't name that file immediately. Take just a few seconds to come up with the best name for it.

He had found a filename that clearly and succinctly described the information it contained. Now whenever he has to find that crucial information about fire codes, he will.

The moral? When naming a file, just *stop to think about it for five to ten seconds.* It is usually the second name you come up with that is the perfect filename. The investment of this negligible amount of time will be repaid many times over in terms of instant retrievability.

TECHNIQUE #18:
Constructive Optimism
Adopt a proactive, "can-do" attitude

How much of your time do you spend being *reactive*, rather than *proactive?* When you work proactively, you are in control—not only of your work, but of your entire present and future, even when you encounter unexpected situations and emergencies. You are excited; you are inspired. Great ideas occur frequently to you as if they dropped out of the sky. These good ideas of yours translate into new projects, as well as new approaches to old projects. The results gratify you and inspire others.

Being proactive means meeting new challenges head-on, not procrastinating until they become crises. Being proactive means diving into your tasks knowing you are going to accomplish them well and on time. It means seeing your Turtle as your personal assistant and thinking, "That's what I'm going to do *next*"—not obsessing about a stack of folders on your desk and falling into despair over what you haven't done. Think about baseball players. In baseball terms, being proactive means stepping up to the plate with confidence, looking the pitcher in the eye, and swinging hard and smoothly into the first good pitch that comes your way. Or think about a young musician challenged by a Rachmaninoff concerto. Only a positive, "can-do" attitude will get that musician on stage to deliver a brilliant performance.

> **Being proactive means meeting challenges head-on and diving into your tasks knowing you will accomplish them well and on time.**

The opposite of being proactive—constantly *reacting* to circumstances that you do not control—means stress. It means inefficiency, perpetually falling behind, and feeling as if you're standing in quicksand. It means chaos.

But that's not you—not now, not any more. You are learning to get your work under control and eliminate the stress. If you manage your information flow according to the lessons in this book, you will replace the negative stress in your life with positive excitement and constructive energy.

Positive discipline

If you were to go out on the street and randomly ask a hundred people to give you their immediate reaction to the word "discipline," what do you think the results would be? I'm willing to bet the majority would give you a negative definition. For many, discipline conjures up images of a harsh schoolteacher, a drill sergeant, a perfectionist of a ballet instructor.

I'm asking you to think about discipline differently. If you think of the ballet instructor, draw the thought out and picture the ultimate results. Discipline is absolutely essential to learning the art of dance. It is essential to competitive sports, music, the martial arts, the practice of medicine, home-building, breadmaking, clock repair, writing software code, meditation, growing up, and everything that is worth pursuing. Discipline is important in overcoming anxiety and depression and, in a certain way, it is necessary for maintaining a sound and happy marriage.

"Discipline" is not a bad word. Discipline should be a positive, creative experience. The only road to achievement is through discipline. The road to spiritual enlightenment, and indeed, the road to freedom—be it physical, mental, or emotional freedom—is through the path of discipline. Discipline challenges us. It calls forth our inner strength.

To be a constructive force, discipline must be aimed positively. This book teaches you to use discipline to manage your workflow. Managing your workflow requires your energy, and the payback is enormous.

See discipline as a *positive.*

In fact, if you really think about it, learning to control your information flow and to maintain an organized, systematic working style requires less energy than living in an *unmanaged*, chaotic state.

Think positively about discipline. Apply your best spirit of discipline to leading an efficient life at work, and the rewards will be unending in your personal and family life as well.

TECHNIQUE #19:
Interruptions
See them in a whole new light and handle them without stress

How often are you interrupted? Your phone rings while you're in the midst of calculating last quarter's expenses. A workmate knocks on your door, needing to see you *now*. A slew of email messages lands in your In-box, and several of them are marked "high priority." How do you deal with any of these?

The first thing you need to understand about interruptions is your attitude about them. How do you feel about interruptions? Are they positive or negative? Most people consider them negative: an interruption is something that gets in the way of something else—I'm doing my work, and the phone rings.

It's important to keep in mind, however, that interruptions are not all 100 percent negative. Actually, you need interruptions. You need those phone calls that bring you important information, inquiries about your services, appointment confirmations, and a million other positive benefits.

Not all interruptions are bad.

When I was a kid, my father was always on my back about something. One day he said to me, "You don't like the fact that I'm bugging you all the time, do you?"

I said, "No."

He said, "There's one thing that would be worse than me bugging you."

I said, "Oh, yeah? What's that?"

He said, "Me not bugging you."

I bring this old memory up because it applies to the subject at hand. The only thing worse than interruptions in your workday is...you guessed it: no interruptions!

In fact, I urge you to stop thinking about interruptions as "interruptions." Instead, think of them as part of your work. Be thankful for those phone calls, drop-ins, and email messages. They mean things are happening—people want to contact you; the work you do or the business you run is thriving.

And let's even take this one step further. Think of a phone call, for example, as a *pause* in what you're doing. Think of it as a potential *opportunity*, or perhaps a *positive challenge*. Someone knocking on your door may be inviting you to a power lunch. That high-priority email may be presenting you with a chance to solve a problem, which means that you might achieve something or make somebody who doesn't know you well respect you for your skill.

Maybe when the phone rings, it is a chance to learn and grow. Even if it's bad news, it may be an occasion for drawing a useful lesson or going more deeply into a personal relationship.

> **What you call an "interruption" may be a positive opportunity.**

In other words, think positively! You may have been calling those unanticipated breaks in your routine "interruptions" and wishing they wouldn't occur, but if you think back about your phone calls, drop-in visitors, and high-priority emails, I'm sure you will find that many of them have presented constructive opportunities. How did you learn about that promotion last year? How will the prospective customer you've been trying to attract let you know you're going to get the contract?

Is this Pollyannaish? I don't think so. A positive attitude will carry you through all sorts of situations in your everyday working life. It's sometimes said that an upbeat attitude attracts positive happenings. I believe that is true. An upbeat attitude can release your creative energy, propel you through challenges, and—by no means least importantly—gain the respect of your fellow workers and superiors.

TECHNIQUE #20:
Next-Step Mentality
Ensure that follow-through is a constant way of life

One of the most valuable attributes for working efficiently is what I call "next-step mentality." To understand next-step mentality, think about how good pool players take their shots. They aren't happy with just sinking a ball; they set up their first shot so that the cue ball will land in perfect position for their next shot; they'll do the same with that next shot, and so on. This is how the game's legendary players, such as Willie Mosconi and Minnesota Fats, always played it. They were champions because they were masters of next-step mentality.

So much for pool; what about business? Let's imagine that I am a sales representative for a hotel. I've just made my biggest sale ever—Maximilien Enterprises, Inc. has booked its annual convention with us for October 3 to 6 of next year, and they are requesting six hundred rooms for their employees and family members. I return to my office and show my sales manager the contract. He orders champagne from the food and beverage department and calls in the sales staff to celebrate.

On April 25, just over five months before the convention, I get a call from Maximilien Enterprises. The person on the other end of the line asks, "How many executive suites did you reserve for our convention?"

My heart jumps into my throat. In my excitement over the contract, I neglected to inform Shelley, our head of reservations, to set aside executive suites. In fact, I'm not even sure Shelley has blocked the six hundred rooms Maximilien Enterprises will be needing.

Oops!

You may think that no conscientious sales rep would make a mistake like that. However, in the excitement of the moment, any one of us is capable of forgetting a follow-up detail, especially if we don't have a mechanism in place that makes it *impossible* for us to omit the follow-up.

In this case, I wasn't operating from a next-step mentality. Ensuring my follow-up would have been simple. All I had to do was to note in my organizer or PDA, the moment Maximilien's CFO was signing the contract, these words: "Shelley—block 600 rooms, incl 9 exec suites." That would have prevented a catastrophe.

The lesson should be clear. Log your very next step. Not only will that give you the pleasure to forget, but you will reap another benefit: simply writing down your next step will automatically stimulate you to think about the step after that step.

Putting next-step mentality into action is a proven, tremendously effective way to seal cracks that important information can slip through.

Monday	*Dec. 18*
Shelly—block 600 rooms incl 9 exec suites	

Figure 18

A Positive, New Approach to Starting Your Day

If you've read through the previous section, you know how much emphasis I place on a positive attitude. I urge you to cultivate within yourself an affirmative outlook on your job, yourself, and your life. This does not mean you have to go around with the kind of overly cheery personality that irritates people by denying problems or hardships; I assume you are a serious person, and you do not trivialize your work or that of others. "Positive" does not mean "bubbly." However, it does imply enthusiasm and optimism.

Performing at your best level requires a constructive approach—and an effective method. Throughout this book so far, I've been describing how to develop both a constructive approach to your job and an effective, systematic way of managing your workflow. In the final technique, we bring it together for that crucial moment of every workday, the moment you step into your office or cubicle and begin the day's tasks. I offer you a tried-and-true procedure that works for the more than seventy thousand people who have successfully applied my methods. For more than three decades, it is what I have taught in seminars, training programs, and consulting sessions around the world.

TECHNIQUE #21:
Your First Four
Morning Tasks
Set yourself up for your entire day

Good morning! Have you inverted your Turtle today? You naturally want to start each day on the right foot. There are four simple yet indispensable steps you can take to make sure every morning begins in a way that sets you up for constructive, creative work and gives you a forward thrust into your remaining tasks. They are outlined in the following paragraphs.

1. Invert Your Turtle

The moment you arrive in your office, take two to three minutes to go through your Turtle and refamiliarize yourself with the tasks in it. Reprioritize them if necessary. The procedure is simple:

1. Take your entire Turtle stack from behind your 180 and place it on your desk.
2. Turn the Turtle stack upside down.

3. One by one, turn each item over, reviewing the Turtle contents sheet by sheet. Ask yourself two questions about each item:

- Is this really a Turtle item, or does it belong in another terminal?
- Is this item in the proper priority within the stack?

4. If necessary, replace each item with the priority you now think it should have. It's possible that nothing will change. On the other hand, it's possible that a memo requiring a reply will move from position number eight in your Turtle to position number two because your input is due shortly; or the deadline for a report has been moved out from today to next week, so that item can be shifted from the number one spot to somewhere farther down your Turtle stack.

Inverting your Turtle refamiliarizes you with your active tasks and shows you the day's priorities.

Note: Be sure to change the Start Date to reflect the task's new priority.

5. When you've completed your review and all items are in their proper priority, replace the stack in the normal Turtle location. Take the top item to your desk.

You will notice that inverting your Turtle serves two purposes: It refamiliarizes you with your active tasks, and at the same time it sets your priorities for the day.

Remember that the Turtle makes it easy for you to add and prioritize new projects or tasks as they come to you during the day.

2. Clear Your Virtual In-Tray

The second thing you should do after arriving at work is to clear your Virtual In-Tray of any materials that have been delivered to you since the last time you were at your desk. Follow the procedure you learned earlier in this book. For each active work item, quickly estimate the time you will need to complete it; write the Completion Date and Start Date at the top of the first sheet, and place the item immediately in your Turtle stack. If it's a large item, fill out a Turtle Sheet and take the item to your Turtle Holding Area, being sure to place the Turtle Sheet in its prioritized place in your Turtle stack. If you have any active work items that can be handled quickly, do it and transfer them either to your Out-Tray or their proper place in your File System.

For other items, remove them from your Vin-Tray and place each in the terminal where it belongs—Pending, Reading, and Trash as appropriate. For more details on handling items in the Vin-Tray, refer back to Technique #3.

3. Process Your Voice-mail

Now it's time to check for phone messages. If you have any, follow the procedure laid out earlier in this book. Use your spiral-bound note-book for writing down the name and number of each caller. Delete each message from your voice-mailbox as soon as you've copied down the necessary information, prioritize the callbacks, and return the calls. Be sure to do the same with any messages you might have received on your cell phone. For details about processing voice-mail, refer back to Technique #14.

4. Process Your Email

Open your email application and download all new messages. Remember—the In-box is your electronic Vin-Tray, so process every message that's in there just as you handle the physical information materials that land on your desk's Vin-Tray. Technique #3 helped you set up folders representing the electronic counterparts to the terminals that hold your paper-based information. (See pages 57–60.) Read the content of each new message, and drag and drop each one into the appropriate terminal.

If a message contains an active task that you can dispatch very quickly, do so; otherwise, drag all active-task messages into your Turtle (ET) folder. Immediately create a Turtle Sheet for each new active task, and place the sheet in its proper priority within your Turtle stack. As an alternative, print out all new active tasks that contain three pages or less; staple them together, write the Start Date and Completion Date on the top page, and place them in the Turtle stack according to their priority ranking.

"Taxi" all other messages to their appropriate email folders—Pending, Reading, Client/Project/Task, Library/Reference, Archive, or Personal. For more information, see Technique #13.

That's it!

When you have completed all of the above tasks and cleared out your In-box, you are ready to turn to the next item of business. Turn to your Turtle stack and pick up your top-priority active task. Place it on your desk, and off you go.

Have a great day. More specifically, have an organized, productive day!

The Integrated Seven Terminals System

From 21 Techniques to an Integrated Working System

Now that you've learned a lot of individual techniques for handling your information flow efficiently, you're ready to take what you've learned to the next level. You're ready to become a virtuoso.

We usually think of a virtuoso as someone who has mastered an art form, the performance of music in particular. However, I like to think of anyone who masters a set of skills or techniques as a virtuoso in his or her endeavors. To become a virtuoso in the art of personal productivity, you need to synthesize what you've learned about the techniques of handling your information flow. Just as virtuosi on the violin or piano are able to put together all their skills and techniques to perform a sonata or a concerto, you should be able to put together the skills and techniques you've just learned to produce a fine-tuned system of work practices.

It all comes together in the Seven Terminals system, an integrated methodology for processing your workflow and really, really maximizing your ability to organize tasks, prioritize them, and get them done on time. The Seven Terminals system enables you to organize items quickly without disrupting the flow of your work. You can prioritize tasks without ever having to make lists again. When all of the terminals are used correctly, no information will ever fall through the cracks and become lost or neglected. You will make far fewer mistakes and omissions in your work, and you will never miss follow-ups.

Put the Seven Terminals system into practice, and you will never have to repeat the purge of your workspace again. Put the system into practice, and you will gain back those hours you've been losing to that bad habit of burning the midnight oil. You'll stop fretting about work you haven't completed, contacts you haven't followed up on, and appointment times you're not sure of. You'll be like Jim, the fellow we met in this book's introduction, who mastered the skills of personal productivity, learned to get control over his workload, and recaptured precious time for family and personal activities. You, too, will find the right balance between your work and your life.

The Seven Terminals System

In Part I, we compared your workspace to an airport where planes land on a runway (your Virtual In-Tray) and are immediately taxied, by you, to a terminal for processing. If you learned all of the techniques described in Part I—especially Techniques #5 and #9 through #12—you have already set up the Seven Terminals in your physical workspace, plus a Virtual In-Tray, or Vin-Tray. Let's review the Seven Terminals now:

- **Trash.** Trash is as simple as it sounds. It is where you put anything you receive or complete that is of no value to you or anyone else, now or in the future.
- **Out-Tray.** Simple again. Your Out-Tray is where you place items to be delivered outside your own work environment.
- **File System.** Your file system is where you keep completed work items. These include file archives and reference material, including contacts and other addresses that you don't store in your computer. It's also where you created a Library for holding newspaper clippings, trade journal articles, and other items containing information you may need.
- **Turtle.** The Turtle is a prioritized active-task repository for all of your work items other than the one project you're working on at the moment.
- **Pending.** The Pending terminal holds items that you cannot go any further with until you receive input from someone else or a scheduled event takes place.
- **Reading.** The Reading terminal holds work-related articles and other items you set aside to read.

- **Personal Organization System.** Your Personal Organization System is where you keep track of dated items, such as appointments and meetings. This may be a paper calendar or an electronic organizer on your computer, a personal digital assistant (PDA), or a book organizer.

Once you've mastered the use of these terminals, you will be ready to handle all of your paperwork with speed and efficiency. Everything that lands on your Virtual In-Tray will go to its proper place, and all of it will be organized and ready for your attention in its proper priority. In addition, you will learn how to manage your business and personal appointments so that you will never forget a meeting or be confused about what is coming up on your calendar.

The electronic terminals

Technique #4 taught you how to set up your computer filing system and your email folders. To a large extent, the folders you created then mirror the Seven Terminals of your physical workspace. You will undoubtedly have noticed some differences, though. It is in your email folders that you hold active task files, in Turtle (ET) and Pending (EP), which come to you via email messages and attached files; and your email In-box is your electronic Vin-Tray.

Technique #13 explained how to use these similarly to how you use your physical terminals, and Technique #15 showed you how the Paper/PC Connection integrates your paper and electronic filing methods. Turn back to those pages in Part I if you'd like to review the electronic functions.

Principles of Information Processing

Just as airport terminals receive planes after they have landed on the runway, the terminals in your office will receive all items of paperwork that arrive in your Virtual In-Tray leaving the Vin-Tray free and clear to receive the next "arrival." An incoming item, like an airplane, must not stop when it lands on your Virtual In-Tray, but must immediately go to its proper terminal. This is true of both paper items that land on your desk and electronic items that land in your email In-box. (To fully review the function of the Vin-Tray and the In-box, please turn back to Techniques #3 and #13 in Part I.)

Some of your office terminals receive items that represent work you must do; others receive items you have worked on and need to move elsewhere—on to another person, for example, into a file, or into Pending. They all serve to organize all of your paperwork and electronic files according to state of activity and priority.

Rule Number 1

Recall this crucial principle as you use the Seven Terminals system: when you're handling an item in your workspace, *do not wait to decide what to do with it.* Implant this rule in your mind.

Think about that airliner landing on the runway. The captain must take it immediately to its terminal. He or she cannot stop on the runway and ponder, "Oh, dear me, what should I do with this 747 and all of my passengers?" If the captain hesitates, the plane will be in the way of the next aircraft coming in for a landing. But don't worry—the captain knows where to take it: off the runway and to the appropriate terminal.

When you use the Seven Terminals system, you will be like that airline captain. You will know what to do with every piece of information, every piece of paper, every bundle of documents that lands on

> **Do not wait to decide what to do with an item that lands in your workspace's Vin-Tray.**

your "runway"—that is, your Vin-Tray. As I promised you earlier in this book, once you absorb the method of the Seven Terminals, you will be able to dispatch incoming information automatically.

Remember that you want to use the Vin-Tray for every item that comes to you. Keep your Virtual In-Tray clearly labeled, as I showed you in Technique #3, and make sure everyone who brings you work items knows to place them only on your Vin-Tray.

Rule Number 2

Any time you can get rid of an item quickly—within, say, sixty seconds, and without losing your focus or concentration—by tossing it, signing it off, or giving it away, then do it quickly. The fewer items you keep, the less work will pile up on you. Whenever an item lands on your Vin-Tray, ask yourself these questions:

- Do I really need this, or may I discard it?
- Is this for me, or should it go to someone else?

No more "To Do" lists

One more thing, while we're on the subject of working principles: Have you noticed that nowhere in my plan is there a "To Do" list?

> **Any time you can get rid of an item quickly, do it.**

That's because you won't be using one ever again. The Seven Terminals system, and particularly the Turtle, takes care of prioritizing for you.

FREQUENTLY ASKED QUESTION

I like my "To Do" list. It gives me something tangible to focus on, and I can check off the items as I finish them. Why do you want me to get rid of my list?

A "To Do" list may work for people who don't have a lot to do, but that's not most of us. For most people, the lists get longer every day. At the beginning of Tuesday, you have leftover items from Monday. At the end of Tuesday, you probably still have leftover items from Monday—plus leftover items from Tuesday. You may also have messy scribbles and crossed-out items. The net effect: your list is growing, not shrinking.

"To Do" lists are cumbersome. Here's an example: Jake sits down every morning and thoughtfully prioritizes his list, only to have new, high-priority tasks come along within the next couple of hours. By noon, Jake has to rewrite the list, and it probably won't be the last time today.

Here are some more reasons why "To Do" lists are not a good idea:

- People who use them have a tendency to think of the first item on the list as the most important, but it might not be at all.
- If you fail to complete the first item on the list, you may be deterred from moving on to the remaining items.
- A "To Do" list has no flexibility; to reprioritize, you have to rewrite the entire list. Even if you use your computer, reordering the priorities wastes time.

Your Turtle: The Center of Your Universe

Okay, I'll admit that it's a stretch to call your Turtle the center of the universe. However, the Turtle is the centerpiece of the Seven Terminals system and the tool that guarantees that you will stay on top of your work priorities. Let's take one more look at what the Turtle can do for you.

The best way to prioritize

There are many problems with using a "To Do" list to prioritize active tasks. Here's an example: At the end of Tuesday, Georgia, a mid-level manager at a software company, wrote out her "To Do" list for the next day, Wednesday. There were seventeen items on the list, including two scheduled meetings, and Georgia carefully listed her non-meeting items in priority order. Almost as soon as she arrived at work on Wednesday, all hell broke loose. The testers in her department found several fatal bugs (defects in the code or routine of a software program) in a product that was scheduled to be shipped the following month. The development lead, the guy in charge of all the programmers, was sick in bed. Meanwhile, Marketing had already sent out a press release with the product ship date prominently mentioned—and now it looked as though that ship date would not be met. Georgia had to spend most of the day putting out fires, and her "To Do" list was toast. She had to rewrite it and shift priorities four times. The reality of Georgia's day had made a shambles of her original, prioritized "To Do" list.

One of the biggest problems with a "To Do" list is that each time you rewrite it, you waste precious minutes and your attention moves away from your highest-priority task, the one you're working on. When it gets this crazy, people will sometimes stop making a "To Do" list—and they won't have anything to replace it. Now their sole objective is to avoid drowning in a sea of uncompleted work at the end of each day.

You avoid this problem by using your Virtual In-Tray and the Turtle. As soon as something arrives on the Vin-Tray, you immediately put down the task item you're working on and quickly assess the new item. If the new item requires work on your part, turn from your desk and put the item into your Turtle *in order of its priority* relative to the other items already there. This process will take only a few seconds, and then you turn back to your desk, instantly regaining full focus on the task at hand.

So let go of your lists and use your new, much-improved tool set: the Seven Terminals system.

Inverting your Turtle

Technique #21 taught you that inverting your Turtle is the very first thing you do in the morning upon coming in to work. Refer back to that technique if you need to, but I want to emphasize it here once more: every morning, the moment you arrive in your office, take the two to three minutes required to go through your Turtle and refamiliarize yourself with the tasks in it, reprioritizing them if necessary. That will get you started on a day during which you will manage your information flow with skill and confidence.

Blocking Turtle Time

There are times when you might find yourself overwhelmed because you are being constantly interrupted when you have a great deal of work to do. This often happens among administrative support staff, managers, and project leads who have to fulfill their own assignments

> **When you need to concentrate and catch up on work, block Turtle Time. Isolate yourself in a place where you can work undisturbed.**

while at the same time supervising team members. If that's you, it's likely that your co-workers are frequently coming to see you or calling you with a question. You are expected to make decisions, sort out disputes, put out prairie fires. And you're also expected to write that report, answer your email, make your sales calls...whatever. How do you do it?

By *blocking Turtle Time*. This means setting aside a certain amount of time to get your tasks done by isolating yourself in a place where you can do it. Arrange to have the use of a quiet room or area, away from the work traffic and noise of your normal day—co-workers, your boss, your telephone—and hole up long enough to catch up with your responsibilities. Make it a place where you have all necessary electronic supports. Let others who might need to see you know how you can be reached in case of an emergency; just make it clear that you need this time and you should not be disturbed unless it is absolutely necessary.

I realize that, for many people, the idea of isolating yourself like this sounds unrealistic—especially if you're not the head of your company. However, when my admin comes to me requesting permission to go off by herself in order to catch up with her work, I never hesitate to say, "Go for it!" After all, my admin is doing *my* work, work that supports me and my company. I see this as a part of the new paradigm of work in the information age, a necessary strategy to work smart, be efficient, and fulfill our goals. Think of it like this: isolating yourself when necessary to complete your work load is what you do in lieu of staying in the office long into the evening or losing much-needed sleep because of worry and anxiety.

I've counseled thousands of administrative support staff who will testify that when they make a practice of blocking Turtle Time, they get at least three times as much done than during the same amount of time at their desks; some say they get an entire day's work done in just a few hours. And I know managers who see the size of their support person's Turtle stack and actually ask them to go into the conference room, or some other quiet place, to work privately. It makes sense— whose work is the support person doing, after all? So if you are hesitant to ask your manager for Turtle Time, remember that it is in everybody's interest that you be able to get your work done.

Blocking Turtle Time applies to everybody, not just support staff. No matter what your job, I guarantee that taking some time to work undisturbed will give you an opportunity to accomplish a lot of what you might not otherwise get done. Your productivity will increase; your Turtle stack will diminish; you will get your reading done. The most important part of it, however, is not the amount of work you will complete; the most important part is how terrific you feel because your stress will be dramatically lowered.

Note: If you don't have the option of stealing away to a quiet room during the workday, another option is to block Turtle Time outside your normal working hours when you are least likely to be disturbed. *I* do not *recommend blocking Turtle Time* after *normal work hours.* Instead, bite the bullet and get into your office e-a-r-l-y. Chances are, your family won't miss you at 6:00 a.m., but they will miss you at 6:00 p.m. Also, you're fresh in the morning and have a clearer head than at the end of the day. Really! It's incredible how much you can accomplish in those quiet hours of the early morning.

Turtle Touchdown!

Would you think I'm nuts if I asked you to imagine leaving work at the end of one day in your life with nothing left in your Turtle? That is, you've completed all of your active tasks up to this moment. This is what I call a "Turtle Touchdown"—and I've trained many, many people who have actually scored one. In fact, I get lots of letters from clients that read like the following:

Score a Turtle Touchdown!

Figure 19

Dear Len,

After seventeen years as an engineer, I have achieved something I never thought possible, thanks to your help. I thought I'd never see the day when I went home at 5 p.m. with all of my active tasks completed. However, I am writing to tell you that I just scored a TURTLE TOUCHDOWN! Hooray! And thank you!

Daniel _____, Sun Microsystems

I promise you that if you follow the teachings in this book faithfully, you will score a Turtle Touchdown at least once in your career. And when you do, write me a letter. I'll send you a *Turtle Touchdown* certificate.

Now, don't expect this to happen all the time. In fact, on the day after your Turtle Touchdown, you may go home with five items in your Turtle. So what? You'll be seeing your work in a whole new light.

Tips & Tricks for Greater Working Efficiency

Soon I'm going to quiz you by running through some of your daily tasks, but first I have two more tips to pass along.

Symbol shortcuts redux

We've already talked about symbols you can use for reminding yourself about the location of certain materials, the content of voice-mail, and the results of phone calls. We also learned about symbols you can use to coordinate your Pending terminal and your Personal Organizer or appointments calendar. The following chart shows a complete list of symbol shortcuts. I recommend that you use these symbols on your Personal Organizer, electronic or paper, to instantly locate information when it comes time to complete pending tasks.

Use this symbol	If the proposal is
(P)	In your Pending terminal
(PHA)	In your Pending Holding Area
(H)	The proposal's "home" file or in your
(EP) (EH)	electronic files (i.e., on your computer)
(P-A)	Being held by your administrative assistant

Working steadily

Finally, I'd like to offer a general piece of advice that applies to every aspect of your job, but especially to the way you handle your information flow: work steadily. It's not a good practice to work in spurts and slack off in between. Over the long term, it is a steady, consistent effort that gets things done.

Think of athletes—a successful athlete is one who uses his or her natural abilities *efficiently:* the powerful golf stroke, the smooth tennis swing, the precise kick of a soccer ball, the perfect coordination in swinging a baseball bat. Endurance sports, such as rowing, swimming, and long-distance running, require constant efficiency over a relatively long stretch of time. If a marathon runner runs in spurts, he or she is not running efficiently and is likely to lose the race.

> **Work steadily. Apply a consistent, positive discipline to your job.**

So, too, with ourselves in our careers. Handling the day-to-day pressures of a twenty-first-century career requires a consistent, steady discipline. People who work on their information-processing tasks in spurts, allowing information to accumulate between bursts of productivity, will not master the workflow and will sink back into old habits that quickly lead back into chaos.

Promise yourself that you won't slip into this negative pattern. You've just learned how to work in a disciplined, productive way. Commit yourself that, from this day on, you will allow my program to support you. You will master your workflow and look forward to every day with confidence.

Applying What You've Learned

Now you know all about the Seven Terminals system as an integrated method of working above and beyond the twenty-one techniques. It's time to see if you're really a virtuoso by applying what you've learned. This chapter will lay out some scenarios and test your understanding of your new working system.

Ready? Here we go.

Good morning. Have you inverted your Turtle?

It's the beginning of your workday, and you've just arrived at the office. You've hung up your coat, sat down at your desk, and switched on your computer. You know you have a full day ahead of you. What do you do now?

If you said, "Invert my Turtle," you were absolutely right. That's what you do. You turn around, behind your 180, pick up your Turtle stack, and place it on your desk. Now turn the stack upside-down on your desk.

Turn the Turtle items over one by one and refamiliarize yourself with each of them. Page through your work quickly, including the Turtle Sheets, yet be very conscious of each item you handle. Consider each task's start date as the key to prioritization.

Now is the time when you reprioritize your Turtle tasks, if necessary. Judging by the Start Date, you should be able to tell immediately when there is a task that needs to be placed in a different priority position. If you get to the middle of your stack and find a task that you need to work on today, you obviously move it toward the top of your Turtle. If you see something near the top of the stack that you don't have to start on until a later date, reposition it in the stack below the tasks that you need to work on sooner.

When you've finished going through your Turtle, check your Virtual In-Tray. If any items have arrived, pick them up one by one and place each in its proper terminal. Assess each item quickly *according to where it belongs in the Seven Terminals system.* If you discover any active work items that belong in your Turtle stack, stop and position them within the stack according to priority *based on the date you must begin the work.*

When you've emptied the Vin-Tray and "taxied" all new items to their proper terminals, turn back once again to your Turtle. Take the single highest-priority item from the top of your Turtle and place it on your desk. This is your first work item for today, and the only item you will have on your desk until you complete it—unless some emergency requires your immediate attention. Now you have the pleasure to forget those other items in your Turtle stack. Their time will come; it's just not now.

> From now on, every workday begins with inverting your Turtle, clearing your Vin-Tray, and processing voice-mail and email.

Okay, you've inverted your Turtle and cleared your Vin-Tray. Before turning to anything else, you should complete two more tasks to start your day right: processing your voice-mail and processing your email. If you don't recall exactly what these tasks entail, turn back to Part I and read the brief procedures for voice-mail and email in Technique #21.

That is how your day begins. Not just today, but every day for the rest of your working life.

Let's look at some scenarios that will illustrate typical workday situations and test what you've learned. Each scenario will represent a quiz, posing one or more questions for you to answer.

While you were out, your Virtual In-Tray...

You've begun your day normally, completing your first four start-up tasks. You've set to work on your top-priority task and made good progress on it, but then you had to go to two back-to-back meetings. When you return to your workspace, you see that your admin has placed five items on your Vin-Tray. Good, you think to yourself, your admin gets it—that's where incoming information goes. Do you feel confident about handling the new items?

#1. You've got a load of work today. Your highest-priority active task is still on your desk, uncompleted, and you've got those five items in your Vin-Tray. You're going to have to check your email and your voice-mail. *What do you do now?*

If you said, "Sort out the items in my Vin-tray and taxi them to their proper terminals," give yourself a gold star. That's exactly what you do. Let the email and voice-mail wait a moment longer. Forget your old paradigm of immediately going back to work on the project that's on your desk (if that's how you used to do it). Instead, pick up the items from your Vin-Tray and deal with them first, taking just a few seconds to place them in their proper terminals. Remember, you've got to keep the runway clear for the next incoming plane (work item).

#2. You pick up the first item from your Vin-Tray and see that it's a letter from the president of Frazer Motors, a client of yours, thanking you for a project you've completed for them and praising your work. *What do you do with it?*

Did you say, "File it"? Good—give yourself another gold star. Your File System is for completed work. You have no more to do on the Frazer Motors project, but you do anticipate more business from them. It's always nice to have a letter from a satisfied client, and this particular letter will now serve as a customer reference. You may want to file it in a file marked "Testimonials" (may this file of yours grow to overflowing). Then move on to the next item in your Vin-Tray.

#3. The next item is a letter for your signature verifying a major change-order for a project that you are supervising. You had the letter

FREQUENTLY ASKED QUESTION
Can you give me some general guidelines about how to prioritize my tasks in the Turtle stack?

Every item in your Turtle stack needs to be started at a particular time. Remember that the Completion Date drives the Start Date; in each case, the Start Date has to be far enough in advance of the Completion Date for you to finish the task on time. And don't forget that life is subject to change without notice, which means you should build some cushion into your time estimates.

When you assign a Start Date, make sure you take account of other tasks you will begin between the Start Date and the Completion Date. For example, let's say you must write a report that is due on Friday, the 30th, and you figure it will take you four days to write the report. That points to the 26th as the Start Date—but wait a minute, you have a slide presentation due on the 29th with a Start Date on the 27th. You may need to move one or the other of those Start Dates earlier if you're going to finish both tasks on time.

It's the *Start Date* that drives the priority of each task in your Turtle stack. Make sure that every active task is positioned within your Turtle according to its start-date-driven priority, earliest Start Date at the top of the stack and latest Start Date at the bottom.

drawn up earlier, reviewed it, and gave it to your admin for a few corrections. These corrections have been made, and you now have in your hands the final copy of your letter on company letterhead. *What do you do with it?*

Do I hear "Sign it and place it in the Out-Tray"? Hey, another gold star for you. Soon you'll be wearing so many gold stars you won't get through the metal detectors at the airport. Perhaps your admin comes in regularly to pick up items from your Out-Tray; if so, just let him or her pick up the letter with your fresh signature. If you don't have an admin, or if the admin doesn't come in before the next time you step out of your office, you may want to take the letter out yourself the next time you leave your office or cubicle.

This signature, which requires only a moment of your time, is exactly the kind of Vin-Tray task that should take precedence over the item that's on your desk. You can sign the letter and move it along quickly without delaying your further work. You will also be doing one of your colleagues a favor by expeditiously returning work that someone else needs to complete.

#4. The next item in your Vin-Tray is a request for proposal (RFP) from Newmark Pens, a prospective client. You're pleased, because you had been "courting" Newmark for some time and hoped they would use your services. Here's your big chance. *What do you do with the RFP?*

Of course, you immediately recognize the task as a Turtle item. First, you need to assess the task's priority. The proposal is due on the 22nd of this month, and you know, from past experience with RFPs, that it will take you three working days to put this one together. That puts your Start Date at the 19th. However, you know that life is uncertain, and so you want to give yourself a cushion; therefore, you make your Start Date the 17th. Today is the 11th, which makes this RFP a medium-level priority item—you don't have to do the work now, but you need to make sure it's in the queue for you to start on the 17th.

> **For every active task, you assess its importance and make sure to place it in your Turtle according to its proper priority.**

You turn to your Turtle stack and look for the RFP's proper position in the middle of your Turtle. There you see an item that has a Start Date of the 16th. You page down one more item in the Turtle stack and see that the next one's Start Date is the 25th, and—*voilà!*—you've found the place for the new item. The Newmark RFP goes on top of the one with the Start Date of the 17th.

Note: The entire process that I have just described should take you no more than fifteen seconds.

#5. The next item you take from your Vin-Tray was sent to you by a vendor. It's a marketing brochure for version 3.0 of an enterprise software package. However, you've already considered this particular software and decided you don't need it and you are never going to purchase it. *What do you do with the marketing brochure?*

Did you say, "I throw it into my 'circular file'"? If so, you're right again. That's what your wastebasket is for. This is a perfect example of something you don't want cluttering up your office space. Trash it. If you have a recycle bin, all the better. In any case, get rid of it now.

See how easy it is to apply the Seven Terminals system? I can tell you're soon going to be breezing through the processes automatically.

Someday you may even be able to handle your information flow in your sleep, but I don't recommend that as a course of action. Okay, I'm kidding about working in your sleep. Your sleep time is important—and now you're going to be able to enjoy it more, resting in the knowledge that you've got your work under control.

Let's move on to the next item in your Vin-Tray.

#6. Your colleague, Tom, has dropped off the budget projections for the upcoming fiscal year of Jespersen Realty, which we mentioned in Technique #11. You were working on a financial statement for Jespersen when you discovered you couldn't go any further because you needed those budget projections. Tom promised to get the information to you by today, and he has come through. *How do you find the Jespersen project materials that you were working on when you put the task aside because you needed further information?*

The Jespersen materials are where you put them: in their "Home"—the File System folder where you keep all of your records for Jespersen Realty. *How do you know you put the materials there and not in the Pending area of your desk drawer?*

Because you logged the Jespersen project in your Personal Organizer for today and added the symbol Ⓗ on the page for today's date (the date Tom told you to expect the budget projections). And what would be the location of these files if they did not have a "Home" in your File System? Your Pending terminal Ⓟ. To review the difference between Pending and "Home," see Technique #10 in Part I.

Good going! But *what do you do with the Jespersen file* now that you have the required information from Tom?

The answer is that this Pending item now becomes a Turtle task. You have all you need to complete the Jespersen financial statement, and now you must put the file where you will find it when it comes time to finish up. You remove the file from its "Home," add the budget information you just received from Tom, and place it in your Turtle.

Where in your Turtle do you place it?

Wherever it belongs as an active-task priority. Treat the Jespersen task just as you treated the RFP from Newmark Pens. (See scenario #4, above.) That is, determine the Completion Date (or deadline), keeping in mind that the *Completion Date drives the Start Date.* Place the active task in your Turtle stack above all items with later Start Dates.

> **A Pending item becomes a Turtle task when you receive all the information you need to complete the work.**

Why don't you complete the Jespersen project now, rather than sticking it away in the Turtle? Because you already have work on your desk that represents your highest priority, and there are more items in your Turtle that are of a higher priority (that is, need to be worked on sooner) than the Jespersen statement.

More work

Just as you finish sorting out those five pieces of work from your Virtual In-Tray, your admin brings you another. No problem—you're on a roll; you can handle that new item quickly.

#7. It's the new edition of the *Journal of Accountancy*. You've been waiting for this; you've heard some buzz about an upcoming article on real estate tax accounting, and you're eager to read it. This is your personal copy of the journal. *What do you do with it?*

You pick it up from the Vin-Tray, open it, and quickly scan the table of contents (TOC). "Aha," you say, "there's that article I was expecting." You clip the pages out of the journal and staple them together. Then you scan the TOC further to see if there are additional articles you want to read, and you clip and staple each one.

Note: It's really best to use staples rather than paper clips, because paper clips can easily become detached or attach themselves to other work. If you don't want to staple the sheets, binder clips (which come in all sizes) are a reasonable alternative.

Where do these clipped articles go?

In your Reading terminal, of course. Place them in the Reading stack in their order of priority relative to the other pieces you intend to read.

What do you do with the rest of the journal?

Toss it out or recycle it. Journals and magazines can become clutter very fast. You do not want to find your space filled with old journals, magazines, and other periodicals that you've never read. Remember the mantra from Part I: *When in doubt, throw it out!*

#8. Now you see one more item in your Virtual In-tray. It's a note from Rebecca, a colleague who stopped by your office while you were in your last meeting. She asks you to call her. *What do you do with the note?*

You treat it just like voice-mail: Take the spiral-bound notebook you use for logging voice-mail, and write "Rebecca" on the next available line. Add to your notation any other important information from Rebecca's note, such as her phone number, the time she stopped by, and the gist of any further message she might have written. Decide where Rebecca fits in terms of your phone-call priorities, and plan to call her as promptly as you can. (Remember that if Rebecca is one of those people with whom you really don't like to speak, you should make her your *first* call. After completing your call to her, the rest of your calls will feel like Nirvana.)

...and your electronic terminals...

Of course, your computer and telephone do not sleep while you're dealing with your paperwork and attending meetings. People are always sending you email, and when you're not at your desk to answer your phone, you're getting voice-mail. The following are a few situations that might resemble some you encounter.

#9. An email message from your cousin Freddy begins with the following: "Hey, did you know about the so-called boarding house our great-aunt Adeline ran in Nevada? Well, it just might not have been a 'boarding house,' after all..." *What do you do with this message?*

Obviously, you want to read it! But it's a long message and you don't have time for it now. You need to move it out of your In-box, though, because—remember?—that's your electronic Vin-Tray and you've got to treat it like an airport runway and keep it clear.

This little bit of family gossip is exactly the kind of email your Personal email folder is for. Move that message from Freddy there, and

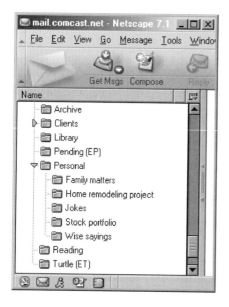

Figure 20

you'll know where to find it when you have a free moment for airing out the family laundry.

Many of us receive jokes or wise sayings that friends send us by email. If you like to keep some of these, that, too, is what the Personal folder is for. In fact, you might want to create subfolders within the Personal folder and label them Family Matters, Jokes, and whatever other categories you design for instant retrievability.

#10. Another of your email messages is from Ellen, in your firm's downtown office, asking you what the state tax department's filing deadline is for a business client you and she both work with. This is a no-brainer that simply requires you to check a state government web page that you've referenced in your Internet Explorer "Favorites" list (or "Bookmarks," if you use Netscape). However, you do have other work to do. *What do you do now?*

If you know you can provide the answer in less than sixty seconds, and without having to shift a great amount of focus and concentration to it, by all means look it up on the web page and send the information in a reply to Ellen. Like the signature we discussed earlier (see scenario #3), this is the kind of small-potatoes task that you want to dispatch immediately and get it out of the way. It won't distract you from anything else you're doing for more than a moment, and by taking care of Ellen's question now, you eliminate having to deal with it later.

> **Take care of small tasks immediately, and you won't have to deal with them later.**

#11. There's an email message from Acme Freight, one of your clients. You open the message and see that the information pertains solely to an agreement Acme had with a third party. It is important information, but it has nothing to do with anything in your current projects. *What do you do with it?*

This email belongs in the appropriate electronic folder for Acme Freight, either in the Acme Client folder or, if you file your records by Project or Task, in the proper subfolder of one of those categories. There is nothing in this email pertaining to an active task. It is not reading material, and it isn't information you were awaiting in order to complete an active task. Because Acme is still an active client, you don't want to archive the message. Your electronic File System is the place for it. Drag and drop the message into the subfolder where you keep information pertaining to Acme Freight. Should you ever need this email, you will be able to retrieve it immediately.

#12. Your next email message is from a representative of your client, Abbott Construction, with an attached file containing information related to tax work from three years ago. It is not something you need to deal with at all. *What do you do with it?*

Frequently Asked Question

Should I use subfolders in my electronic filing system?

Subfolders in your electronic (computer) files can be a good idea. It should not be difficult to tell if you need them. Let's say, for example, that you have an Archive folder with only ten files in it, all pertaining to clients you no longer deal with (and do not expect to deal with again). With only ten files to look at, it's easy to see at a glance what's in that folder. However, if you have a large number of files in the Archive folder, it makes sense to create subfolders labeled according to client names or, perhaps more appropriately, subject matter.

For Client, Project, or Task folders, you will usually find it useful to create a second, and maybe a third, level of subfolders, especially if you accumulate files and email on numerous topics. (See example below.) However, it's important to keep your subfolders limited to two or three levels at most. Too many levels of subfolders can cause confusion when you're trying to locate a specific file.

Example:

🗁 Acme Freight
    🗁 Financial statements
        🗀 Current year
        🗀 Previous years
        🗀 Legal & contract
    🗁 Tax records
        🗀 2005
        🗀 2004
        🗀 Previous years

The message goes into the Archive folder. This is the place where you store information that is of no practical value at this time and will probably never be, unless it is needed someday for legal, tax, documentation, or government purposes. You archive the message rather than deleting it, because you figure that the tax information should be kept.

#13. Now you open an email message from Chris in Human Resources, who has sent a file attachment. It's a spreadsheet with the company's projected personnel budget for the next two quarters. Chris asks you to fill in some data about your department's needs. *What do you do with this message?*

You drag it into your Turtle (ET) folder and immediately create a Turtle Sheet (on paper!) for the active task. Put the Turtle Sheet in your Turtle stack according to its priority relative to other active tasks. Remember that its priority is driven by the Start Date, which, of course, you enter on the Turtle Sheet. Be sure to give the task a clear, distinctive title, such as "Personnel Data for HR," and write Ⓔ in the "Location of Information Needed" field. Now you have something in your Turtle—the familiar Turtle Sheet—to represent the active task that resides in your computer (ET).

Be sure to fill out that Turtle Sheet immediately. If you don't do it immediately, someone could stop by your office and pull you out for a coffee break, or your phone could ring and you learn of a brush fire requiring you to run to an impromptu meeting. If you don't get the active task logged on a Turtle Sheet, the file you've just moved into your electronic Turtle goes into an electronic black hole. You won't have a reminder of it in your physical Turtle—or anywhere else—and if there is a deadline involved, you could very easily miss it.

This is what the Seven Terminals are all about: saving you from lost information, missed deadlines, and the stress of not being sure you have it all under control. Form the right habits now. Log that electronic file as an active task on a Turtle Sheet, and you'll be certain to work on the task when it's time to do so.

#14. Here's an email message that's something to get excited about. It's from Suzanne of the speakers' bureau, telling you you've been invited to be guest speaker at an industry conference. The date has not been confirmed, but it will be three months from now, on either the 13th or the 14th. Suzanne asks if you are interested and says she will get back to you on the 2nd of next month with a confirmed date. This

FREQUENTLY ASKED QUESTION
What's the rule about when to knock out an active task immediately as opposed to putting it in the Turtle?

If you can handle the task within sixty seconds and the item requires little concentration, do it. If the new task is going to take more time and requires a focus that will keep you from getting right back into the work you're currently doing, put the new task in your Turtle and prioritize it. The point is that you want to dispatch an item immediately if you can—but not at the cost of disturbing the rhythm of your current, top-priority work

You will soon develop the ability to judge instantly which active tasks can be handled immediately.

is something you definitely want to do, and both of the possible dates are free on your calendar. *What do you do?*

First of all, you reply to Suzanne by email, saying you are available on either of those dates and telling her you will look forward to her informing you of the confirmed date by the 2nd of next month. Second, you save Suzanne's message in your electronic Pending ⓔ𝓟 folder, by either dragging and dropping the message into the EP folder or using the *File > Save As* command from the menu of your email application. Third, you note on your Personal Organizer (appointments calendar, paper or electronic) on the 2nd of next month that you expect Suzanne's confirmation then, and add the ⓔ𝓟 symbol at the left of your calendar note. Finally, make two notations on your Personal Organizer, one on the 13th and one on the 14th of the month when the conference will be held, so that you will keep those dates clear for your speaking engagement. (If you're using a paper-based organizer, write these two notations in pencil. You might add a question mark to help you remember that the dates are unconfirmed.)

Do you see how this works? You've covered all bases quickly and thoroughly. On the 2nd of next month, your Personal Organizer will show you that you're expecting Suzanne to confirm the date, and you've kept both alternative dates clear. When the 2nd rolls around, you will see that the original email is in your EP folder; this is your guaranteed reminder to nudge Suzanne if she overlooks contacting you.

> **Make effective use of your Personal Organizer terminal together with Pending work, and nothing will fall through the cracks.**

When she confirms the exact date of your speech, you will delete the alternative date that you were tentatively holding. Nothing falls through the cracks.

Now you see that you've cleared all email messages from your In-box. By continuing to process your email like this, you will have an empty In-box when you leave work at the end of this day—and every day. Now that's something to celebrate!

#15. Just now, one of your workmates, José, pops his head in your door and tells you about an important article he found on the Web about a new rule concerning tax shelters. José tells you how to find the article and returns to his desk. The information sounds like something you need to know about, but you don't have time to read the article today. *What do you do?*

This one is quick and easy. You save the web article in your electronic Reading folder. With your browser open to the first page of the article, click *File > Save As* (or, in *Netscape, File > Save Page As*) and click through your folder directory to save the page in your electronic Reading folder. Print the first page and place it in your Reading stack.

If you prefer, you can instead print all of the web pages you want to read and add them to your paper Reading stack. Whichever method you choose, put the paper(s) in the stack according to their priority relative to other reading materials you've collected there.

#16. For the final scenario, let's suppose that you are an attorney with a large law firm. You receive an email message from Bolder and Brash, another law firm, presenting a contract for a business merger involving one of your clients. You are asked to review the contract.

FREQUENTLY ASKED QUESTION
How often should I check my email?

The answer depends on your working style and the volume of email you receive. At a minimum, you should check your messages at least four times a day at established intervals. If you don't, you could miss getting timely information about a meeting, a change in plans for a project, or some other important business. Most of us are in the habit of checking email more frequently. When at my computer, I check for messages approximately every thirty minutes. For sure, if you get a hundred, two hundred, or more messages daily, you have to check them more frequently than a few times a day or you will fall hopelessly behind. The good news is that with your new Seven Terminals system, you will be processing your email rapidly and effortlessly.

Simply keep in mind that your *In-box is the electronic version of your Virtual In-Tray*, and your objective is to keep it clear. Obviously, you cannot answer each and every email as soon as it arrives, and you shouldn't try to answer them all every time you check your In-box. However, you should make it your goal to move messages out of your In-box and into your electronic terminals—the Archive, Clients (or Projects or Tasks), Library, Pending (EP), Personal, Reading, and Turtle (ET) folders—as soon as you can. Be sure to delete all messages that do not pertain to you, need no reply, or contain no information you can use now or in the future.

Make it your goal to go home at the end of every day with an empty In-box. You will be astounded as this becomes a reality.

The contract is attached to the email. You review the contract and find it to be in order. In fact, you admire the way contract is drawn up and believe it might be useful as a template for similar contracts you will write in the future. *What do you do with it?*

You have several options. First, you can save the message in your electronic Library folder so that you have it in an easily accessible place for future reference. If there is nothing of future value in the email message, you might want to save just the attached file (the contract itself) in your Library folder. A third alternative is to save the attached file in the Library folder and save the email message in the appropriate Client folder.

Now you're on your own

The exercises in this chapter have given you a taste of how the Seven Terminals system works, including the electronic components of the system. You can see what I meant at the beginning of this book when I said it's not the *amount* of information that was causing chaos in your work, it was the *lack of an efficient system* for managing the information. The longer you apply my system, the more you will experience the pleasure of having your stress dramatically reduced because you are on top of your information load. And the more you stay on top of your work load, the more quality time you will gain for the things in life you really want to enjoy: more family activities, hobbies and personal-enrichment activities, volunteer work, culture, sports, travel, meditation...whatever you've been dreaming of. That's what we'll talk about in the final section of this book.

PART III
TRANSCENDING
THE WORKDAY
WORLD

Your Dreams
and Goals
Becoming
Reality

Now that you've learned how to overcome the chaos of clutter and maximize your personal productivity, it's time to transcend your workday world and concentrate on improving your quality of life. What are your life goals? What gives you pleasure? What fulfills you? What activities do you want to give more of your time to, and who are the people you want to be more involved with? These are the questions that ultimately define us as human beings.

Who can focus on life goals while totally preoccupied by the chaos at work? No one. However, once you've gained control of your working life, you can easily find the time, energy, and focus to seriously pursue your dreams. And that is the essential ingredient in restoring a positive balance between your work and your life.

Be Realistic and Unreasonable

Several times earlier in this book, we talked about being proactive at work. Now we can talk about regaining a proactive *life*. Do you want to coach your child's soccer team? Vacation in the Mediterranean? Give more of your time and talents to community or faith-based organizations? Take yourself and your family fishing, hiking, sailing, or skiing? Take night classes? Improve your golf or tennis game? Read the great literary classics? Dig out that old guitar from the attic and tune it up again? Build in time for daily meditation, or go off on a spiritual retreat? Learn a new language? Write the great American novel?

You probably don't need a lot of help thinking about the possibilities for an exciting, proactive life. But how do you go about actualizing it? How do you set goals and structure your approach to achieving them?

This concluding chapter offers a simple and effective method for capturing dreams and ideas, fashioning them into exhilarating goals, and—best of all—realizing them. I challenge you to the pursuit of goals that are realistic, yet unreasonable. Yes, that's right, I said *unreasonable*—unreasonable in the sense that, by pursuing those goals, you will break old habits and push yourself to a higher level of enthusiasm and commitment than you previously thought possible.

Fear of Backsliding?

Before we sail into that great future, let's talk about how to deal with one potential hang-up. Once in a while, it does happen that someone will start out using my techniques, see them work for a while, and then slip. Maybe they neglect the routine of inverting their Turtle first thing in the morning. Possibly they aren't logging all the necessary Pending information, or they let email accumulate.

If you should find yourself backsliding, my first piece of advice is this: don't focus on what you may be doing wrong, focus on what you're doing right. Step back for a moment and think about how you've learned your productivity tools and applied them. Acknowledge yourself for how far you've come, and appraise the effectiveness of the techniques you're using. Have you seen an improvement in your working efficiency? Are you able to keep important details from falling through the cracks, and are you making fewer mistakes? Do you sense a greater degree of creativity in your work? Have you experienced a considerable reduction in stress? If you see an improvement in any of

> Acknowledge what you're doing right, and then return to what's causing the problem.

these areas compared with how you worked before applying your new techniques, be aware of this.

Now let's return to whatever it is that's causing you a problem. What is it? Step back and look at your working pattern, as if from a distance, and ask yourself, "Exactly which part of the program am I not applying fully?" Is it that:

- I am not immediately emptying the materials in my Virtual In-Tray and taxiing them to their proper terminals?

If that's where my problem is, I simply need to take the moment necessary to employ the system and make it work. I must remind myself that, really, it only requires a few seconds to move each item from my Vin-Tray, and committing this tiny portion of my day will reward me with the wonderful peace of mind that comes from knowing I have my information flow under control. I need to remember that it's not the *amount* of work that drove me nuts; it was the *mismanagement* of it. And that, for me, is a thing of the past.

- I am running behind in my Turtle tasks?

If that's the case, it's time to *block Turtle Time*—a time for working with no one around to disturb me: no phones ringing, no workmates dropping in to chat. I should review the discussion of blocking Turtle Time on pages 177–179, because I know I can get three times as much done when I work undisturbed.

Note: Staying late yields minimal results. You're likely to be tired and stressed from the day. Come in early when you're fresh and re-energized.

- *I can't find Pending materials?*

I must be sure to log every "Pending" item in my Appointments

FREQUENTLY ASKED QUESTION
I'm always falling behind on my reading. How can I keep up with it?

Everyone I know has trouble keeping up with his or her reading. We are deluged by reading material. This is why it makes sense to prioritize the materials in your Reading terminal, just as you prioritize your Turtle stack. Put your highest-priority readings on the top of the stack and the lowest-priority readings on the bottom. If you never get to the materials on the bottom, get rid of them—especially if their content is no longer of value to you.

Make the best use of the time you now have available for keeping up, or catching up, with your reading. Before you head to the airport on a business trip, pick up your Reading stack and plan to use that in-flight time to catch up. If you commute to work by bus, train, or subway, use the time for reading.

I myself often intentionally postpone reading certain things in my Reading terminal until my next business trip. Postponing is not the same as procrastinating, particularly when the postponement of a task is intentional and rational. It is, in fact, a consistent habit of mine to accumulate reading and take care of it in flight.

terminal (electronic or paper-based) with the proper symbol designating the location of the task items: ⓟ for the Pending area in my desk drawer, Ⓟ Ⓗ Ⓐ for my Pending Holding Area, Ⓗ for the material's "home" in my File System, Ⓔ Ⓟ or Ⓔ Ⓗ for my electronic files, or Ⓟ-Ⓐ if my admin is holding the materials. If necessary, I should review the sections that lay out the process for handling Pending task items.

- My Reading stack is constantly growing?

I really need to consider coming in to work an hour early just two days each week and reserving that extra time specifically for reading. I should close my door or head for an empty conference room so I can concentrate fully and read thoroughly.

In sum, if you're having a problem, analyze the situation. Figure out exactly which technique isn't working well, return to the chapter in this book that discusses it, and apply the instructions exactly. Your problem will be resolved.

Most importantly, *stay committed to the program.* Have faith in the techniques I've taught you—and *have faith in yourself.* Remember that I've taught many thousands of people to use the Instant Productivity Toolkit, and they have proven its success. You will prove it for yourself, too.

Defining Your Goals

Now we come to the part that's the most fun. You've purged your workspace, set up the Seven Terminals system, and put it all into operation. You're working smoothly and, just as I promised you, far more efficiently than ever before. So efficiently, in fact, that you are able to end your workdays at a normal hour and your weekends are free.

What a luxury, to have such freedom! Now what will you do with it?

Capturing your dreams and ideas

Building a future based on your true life goals begins with thinking, dreaming, and imagining all that you'd like to do and be. Let's start by considering the great thoughts and ideas you already have. Don't be modest; you may not be aware of the many brilliant thoughts and inspirations that continually pop into your head. Many of them get lost because you haven't been given the opportunity to capture them.

If you're like me, some of your best ideas occur either while you're in the shower or while you're sleeping. Perhaps you wake up knowing you've just dreamed about something that could be put to use—and then you fall back to sleep. In the morning, you remember that a great idea woke you in the middle of the night, but you can't remember what it was. Something similar happens to those brainstorms in the shower. Between the time an idea hits you and the time you dry yourself off and start thinking about what to do with it, you have dropped the soap, wiped shampoo out of your burning eyes, and adjusted the water temperature a couple of times. As for that brilliant notion, well, it went gurgling down the drain.

> Building a future based on your true life goals begins with thinking, dreaming, and imagining.

Other situations in which you might be struck by profound thoughts are commuting to work on the freeway, in the workout room, wandering through a fragrant rose garden on your lunch break, or walking through an art museum. It's usually not convenient to stop what you're doing and write an essay on the theme of your new idea, but you can carry a pocket notebook or a personal digital assistant (PDA) to capture the inspiration so that it doesn't slip away from you forever.

I know some writers who always carry a pocket notebook with them for the very reason that story ideas, observations of people and situations, and settings are constantly playing themselves out,

FREQUENTLY ASKED QUESTION

Do you have any special tricks or tools that you use to capture your ideas?

I have two tools that some might consider out of the ordinary. First, I have a flashlight pen that I keep, along with a pad of paper, on my bedside table. If you're not familiar with the flashlight pen, it's no bigger than a regular ball-point pen, but it has a built-in light. It's a great tool that you can use in the middle of the night without having to turn on a lamp.

Second, I keep an old-fashioned grease pencil available in the shower. I can use it for scribbling an idea on the shower wall. When I've finished showering, I copy the idea into my notebook or PDA. (It's easy to remove the greasepaint from the shower wall with a tile cleaner.)

and the writers need to jot down what they see, hear, and smell, along with their own impressions and moods, as "raw material" for their work. You, too, can profit from such a habit to trap your many inspirations.

A PDA is a great substitute for the pocket notebook. Always carry it with you—"Don't leave home without it," in the words of the familiar ad—and employ it to capture your bright ideas and inspiring thoughts.

Whether you use a pocket notebook or a PDA, take down just enough of each idea to serve as an effective reminder. Chances are you don't have time to interrupt whatever you're doing long enough to expand the idea to its ultimate conclusion; leave that for later. Just be sure to retrieve these ideas from your notebook or PDA. At the right time, write them out more fully.

Later in this chapter, we'll talk about one specific way of using this inspiration-capturing strategy.

From Idea to Goal

A goal always begins with an idea, a concept, or at least a vague inkling of what *can be*. Take a moment now to think of just one idea you've had that would thrill you if it became a reality. Maybe it's about starting a book club. Maybe it's about remodeling your home. It could be taking a college extension class to learn Spanish, developing your skills in photography, building your own website, doing your own car repairs, or learning *ikebana*, the wonderful Japanese art of flower arrangement. Perhaps you have even bigger dreams about changing careers, starting your own company, or becoming more deeply involved in service to your community or the world.

Maybe your idea is about strengthening your marriage or improving your love life, getting to know your kids—*really* getting to know them—or firming up your relationship with your parents.

I want to support you in taking these ideas, whatever they are, and converting them into goals, then a plan of action, and finally your reality.

Do you know what the difference is between *dreaming* and *doing*? The answer is simple: *dreaming* requires no commitment on your part; *doing* requires you to commit yourself to a goal, plan your course of action, and *act on it*. All of us

> Dreaming doesn't require a commitment on your part. *Doing* does.

dream; unfortunately, however, not everyone has the courage and determination to take action when the opportunity arises. But you have—or else you wouldn't have read this far in this book.

How can you move from dreaming to doing?

Step 1: Appraise your objective

The first step is to appraise your objective. I want you to be satisfied that your goal meets several criteria. Your goal must be:

- Specific
- Measurable
- Time-framed
- Realistic, yet unreasonable

Let's take a look at these criteria. Goals must be *specific*, because when a goal is vague, it is vulnerable to failure. Jane, a friend of mine, once told me, "My goal is to find a man with whom I can have a relationship." Not very specific, is it? And indeed, Jane kept meeting men who didn't measure up to her standards, whatever they were. I pointed out to her that with each man she met, she was in fact accomplishing her goal: she was having a relationship with him, whether it was just a handshake and a "How-do-you-do" or a three-month romance that failed. I advised her to be more specific about what (and whom) she was looking for. She thought about it and then recognized that she was looking for someone who was considerate, loving, intelligent, sensitive, and open to making a lifetime commitment. Guess what? Jane met the man within three weeks. Today, they are happily married.

Goals must be *measurable*, or else you might never be sure you've achieved what you set out after—or, what's just as bad, you might let yourself settle for less than what you really want. Do you want to make more money? Fine, but *how much* more do you want to make? Set your sights in dollar terms: "I want to make $10,000 a year more than I made last year," or "I want to double my gains in the stock market."

So far, these goals—making $10,000 per year more or doubling your stock-market gains—are incomplete. They need to be *time-framed* if they are to be real. By when do you want to be making $10,000 more per year? If you don't frame that objective within a time span, it isn't very meaningful; you could get to that point twenty years from now and, given normal inflation rates, you'd be pulling in less in real terms than you are now. Give it a specific time frame: "*By June 30 of next year*, I want to be earning $10,000 more than I made last year." The same is true of your stock-market gains: "*By this exact date next year*, I want to have doubled the gains I made last year."

Being specific, attaching measurable standards to your goal, and giving yourself an exact time frame within which to reach your mark will transform a vague and blurry dream into the outlines of an action plan.

And now we come back to that puzzling concept I introduced at the beginning of the chapter: that your goal should be *realistic*, yet *unreasonable*. I consider these criteria to be the keystone of your future ambitions. Perhaps you've long dreamed about running in your local marathon. You're in good physical condition, and you have faith in your ability to do it. That makes your goal realistic. However, you haven't trained for running 26 miles and 385 yards; the longest you've ever run is a 10K (6.2 miles). You've simply never made the time to do the proper training; you've never committed yourself to the challenge. That's what makes this goal of running the marathon unreasonable.

> Being specific, using measurable standards, and setting an exact time frame will transform a vague and blurry dream into an action plan.

However, now your life is different. You've boosted your productivity at work and given yourself more free time. In the words of the Nike commercials, *just do it!* Now you can find the time to train properly. Set yourself a specific accomplishment goal, such as running the marathon in four hours or less without injury (a very important specific!), and set your time frame—for example, next year's marathon. Now there's a goal—specific, measurable, time-framed, and both realistic and unreasonable. Go for it!

Step 2: Understand what it means to really *do*

Do you remember what I said about the difference between dreaming and doing? *Doing* requires you to commit yourself to a goal, plan your course of action, and act on it. The second step in your journey from dreaming to doing is to recognize that "doing" is more complex than it seems. You can do and do and do, but if you don't have a good plan, all of your doing won't accomplish much. If your goal is to run the marathon, you can jog around the park two or three times every week, but you still won't be in shape to run 26+ miles on the day of the event. You need a training plan that's carefully thought out, and you need to follow that plan with an unshakable commitment to it for as long as it takes to get your body, mind, and spirit properly prepared. Similarly, if your goal is to learn Spanish, you can read a textbook, listen to tapes, and drink your fill of margaritas, but you won't learn Spanish well unless you pursue it in an active, structured, and disciplined way.

Step 3: Visualize the end result

By now, I hope I've convinced you to think in specific terms about what it is you are seeking. Now I want to add another dimension:

Don't just *think* about it; *see it.* Picture your idea as a reality. If you don't have a clear *picture* of what you're doing and where you're headed, you will go around in circles without ever getting there. If your goal is to redesign your yard into a beautifully landscaped garden, you need to have a very good visualization in your mind's eye of how it will look when you've completed your garden. If your goal is to spend your vacation time next year on a volunteer project with an archeological team in Peru or an ecological research expedition in Guatemala, you need a clear concept of the end result.

Do you want to take an around-the-world cruise? Visualize this: a huge ocean liner on the open seas, a comfortable stateroom, a port of call in Kingston, Jamaica; passing through the Panama Canal, and more ports of call in Acapulco, Honolulu, Singapore, Bombay...wherever your dream ship takes you. If you have no idea what those places look like, page through brochures, travel

> **Visualization sets the stage for the production of your goal.**

books, and websites with photos. Place yourself in the picture. There you are, mesmerized by the lights of Hong Kong as you glide into port. That's you in the marketplace of Dar es Salaam, bargaining with a vendor for a beautiful, hand-woven cloth.

Or is it your dream to make the world's most delicious pastries? Picture it. Visualize yourself presenting perfectly baked Napoleons to twelve dinner guests. Can you see yourself icing a masterful Viennese torte? Taking three hundred miniature cream puffs you've just baked and filled, and stacking them together into a scrumptious pyramid using melted toffee for mortar?

No matter what your dream is, picturing it helps immeasurably. Spend some energy on the exercise. Pick a time and a place without distractions. Sit down in a comfortable chair, feet flat on the floor with your hands unclasped. Close your eyes, and let the picture form itself in your mind. Paint a mental image of the end result—the reality you want to create. Believe me, the power of visualization is remarkable. It sets the stage for the production of your goal.

Do you see it? If so, you've got a true goal. As you move into the next step, keep visualizing that end result; keep the picture shining brightly in your mind. Now you're ready for the all-important *planning* phase. This will be fun, and it will get you going on the road to achieving your end result.

From Goal to Plan

The best way to convert your goal to a plan starts with a Goal Action Sheet. Take one blank sheet of paper, either letter size or legal size. (Feel free to use additional sheets if you need to.) Write down the goal you're going to pursue. Take as many lines as you need to define the goal, making sure that it is specific, measurable, time-framed, and realistic yet unreasonable. You may use Figure 21 as a model, with the target date defining your time frame. Consider the target date as the culmination, the date when you will achieve your goal completely, and when you fill it in, choose a date that is, like your goal itself, realistic but unreasonable—that is, you fully believe you can meet the timeline, even though you may have to "push the envelope" to make it. Trust yourself—you can do it.

Describing the goal

As you describe the goal, do not spare words. On the contrary, write as if you're writing a letter to your best friend. Be informal and

GOAL ACTION SHEET

Goal:
☐ specific ☐ measurable ☐ time-framed ☐ realistic, yet unreasonable

_____

_____

_____

_____

_____

Target Date: _____

Personal Reward:
What achieving my goal will mean for me

_____

_____

_____

_____

Action Steps:
Brain-dump of effective & expedient steps that will propel me toward achieving my goal

- _____
- _____
- _____
- _____
- _____

Figure 21

conversational; there's no pressure on you. It's best to use complete sentences; that will help focus your thoughts on the specifics of the goal and keep them from sounding like a laundry list. Including visual details is essential. Close your eyes to bring back the images you saw during your visualization exercise, and translate that picture into words as best you can. Use adjectives to make the picture vivid, and verbs to make it active. By all means, express how you feel about the goal you're after. For example, I wouldn't recommend writing, "I want to play the guitar like I used to," but rather, "I want to rediscover the passion I once felt with each string of my guitar."

Use the checklist (*specific, measurable, time-framed, and realistic-yet-unreasonable*) to stay true to the four criteria for defining your goal. **Note:** If you describe your goal in just a few lines, you may not be making it specific, measurable, or visual enough. Draw more out of yourself. Keep writing until you're excited by what you've written.

Personal reward

Note the heading "Personal Reward" on the Goal Action Sheet. This section is all about what's in it for *you yourself:* what benefit(s), satisfaction, or personal gain you will derive from achieving your goal. Is it material reward? Fame? Better health or physical fitness? Having more fun? A stronger sense of love and compassion? Enhanced self-esteem? Greater self-discipline? Be specific, and please observe the following guidelines for describing your personal reward:

- Focus on the benefits you *personally* will gain.
- Use at least three sentences to fill in this section.

Don't be shy about focusing on yourself (first guideline). Nobody is going to accuse you of being selfish or greedy. Remember that the whole idea is to turn your dreams into reality.

Negativity is a no-no in this exercise. You should not, for example, write that your personal reward is, "My children will stop fighting with each other," or, "I'm going to tear down that ugly fence so I won't have to look at it any more." Better alternatives are, "I'm going to be a more compassionate, sensitive parent and encourage my kids to respect each other," and, "A new wrought-iron fence around the front yard will keep the dog in and also be a pleasure to look at every day."

> Focus on what you
> want, not on what you
> *don't* want.

Do you see the difference? Negativity deflects your energy from a healthy vision and disempowers you. Expressing the reward in terms of a positive vision will excite you and draw you forward. Keep your eyes on the prize, as the saying goes; focus on what you *want* to see in your future, not on what you *don't* want.

Action Steps

Now we come to the action-oriented part of the exercise. Sharpen your pencil. What are the actions you're going to have to take to realize your goal?

Treat this section as a "brain-dump." Don't twist yourself into a knot trying to reason your way through the steps. Just relax and let the ideas pop into your head, writing them down immediately. Start each step description on a new line, and don't worry about chronological order for now. You should easily be able to imagine at least a half-dozen Action Steps without giving it much thought.

One way to begin this part of the exercise is by writing down the steps you're most looking forward to. For example, if your goal is to learn the sport of rowing, the first (and most enjoyable) steps you list might be:

- Watch a crew race and carefully observe how the rowers do their work
- Browse websites about rowing
- Personally check out boats down on the lake
- Talk to rowers about why they love their sport and how they got into it

From there, you can start to think more about the further steps necessary, such as asking around about how to find a good rowing instructor, searching the yellow pages, and interviewing rowing instructors by telephone or in person. Again, don't worry about writing these steps down in the right chronological order—just "brain-dump."

If you're tempted to evaluate or judge what you put on the page, don't succumb to the temptation. Just let your ideas flow right out of your head and onto the paper. Write down every thought you have, no matter how nutty it may seem. Remember that you are trying to be unreasonable in your goal-setting, so why not also be unreasonable when thinking about the Action Steps you're going to take? Relax and make this a thoroughly positive exercise.

And don't be discouraged if you get stuck. You might find that those first half-dozen or so steps come spilling out of your mind effortlessly...and then nothing more comes to you. That's okay. It's only temporary. Get up, walk around the room, take a drink of water. Return to the visualization step, and let your brain enjoy its picture of the end result. Then go back and write down any new Action Steps that occur to you.

You will feel the momentum building. You will have written nine steps, eleven steps, or whatever number, and the process will begin to feel automatic. Psychologically, it's akin to visualizing a yellow Volkswagen Beetle. If you close your eyes and picture a yellow Beetle—and you do this often enough—pretty soon you'll be seeing more yellow Beetles in reality than you ever thought there were. You haven't made those Beetles appear just by thinking about them; they were there all along, but now you're conditioned to notice them. So, too, with your action plan. The more you focus on envisioning the steps to your goal, the more they will appear to you, clearer, more detailed, and ever more compelling. You'll think of something while crossing through a public square, and again while you're listening to a Mahler symphony or watching a baseball game on TV, while shopping for a new party dress or hoisting a beer with the guys.

Remember now what we said earlier in this chapter about capturing your ideas? You don't want to let your Action Steps slip away from you as they occur. Carry your pocket notebook or PDA so you can capture them. If you're driving your car or doing something else that requires your full concentration, find a way to pause what you're doing. Pull off to the side of the road, if you have to. Step out of the shower for a moment (or keep that grease pencil handy). Keep that flashlight pen and pad of paper on your bedside table for those dream-inspirations. Again, don't bother to compose a complete essay when the idea hits you (unless, of course, you have the time to do so). It's only necessary to write down the gist of the idea so that you will be able to expand on it later.

Don't browbeat yourself if you don't have your notebook or PDA with you when an idea for an Action Step hits you; just find a usable substitute. You've undoubtedly heard stories about how many grand designs started with a sketch on a restaurant napkin. Don't laugh— scribble on that paper napkin if you have to! Some people find the best method is to leave a message on their own voice-mail.

When you return to your Goal Action Sheet, immediately transfer the notes you've taken or the message(s) you've left for yourself.

Pretty soon you'll have a list of steps that add up to a complete action plan. Now is the time to start making chronological sense out of your list.

Putting it all in sequence

Along the left margin of your Action Steps, number them according to their practical sequence as you see it now. The first step is number 1, the second step 2, and so on, until all of your steps are numbered.

As you're doing this, you may think of additional steps. For example, if your steps to learning how to row include #7, Interviewing rowing instructors by telephone or in person, and #8, Choosing a rowing instructor, it may occur to you that you need an intermediary step, Narrowing the candidates to two. Write in the new step as #7-A.

Note: You may prefer to do this exercise with a word processor rather than on a notepad. If so, you can use the automatic numbering feature to keep your steps numbered in order. Your steps will be automatically sequenced as you move them into their correct positions.

Similarly, you might find some steps that made sense as you were brainstorming them, but now you realize they aren't necessary. You can simply delete them.

In addition, it may make sense for you to take some steps simultaneously. Just give them adjacent numbers (for example, #11 and #12).

Finalizing your plan: Dates

When you've got all of your Action Steps numbered in chronological sequence and you're satisfied (for the moment) that you haven't left any necessary step out, you can then start assigning dates. You'll use the same skill you bring to bear when prioritizing Turtle items. You need to have a clear idea of how much time each step will require.

Be willing to stretch yourself.

Be sure to take into consideration other commitments falling between steps. Once again, be realistic—but be unreasonable. Assign dates you believe you can meet, yet be willing to stretch yourself to accomplish what might not seem reasonable according to your old life's paradigms.

As you did with your Turtle items, set a date for the completion of each Action Step. You're making a commitment to yourself to achieve your goal by your targeted date, so you really want to stay on schedule. The greater your commitment to that date, the more smoothly everything else will fall into place and the better you will feel about the process.

Making intelligent and realistic estimates of the time each step will take will help you break your assigned dates down further into a Start Date and a Completion Date for each Action Step. It's likely that some of your steps can be completed on the same date you start them, while others may take more than one day.

Once you have all of your dates assigned, you should coordinate these dates with your Appointments terminal. *Log these dates onto your paper or electronic calendar* so that you have a continuum of support. This will ensure that you do not fall behind because of having overlooked an Action Step at the scheduled time.

From Plan to Action

Little remains to be said about how to achieve your goal. Now it remains for you to *do* it. Use your Goal Action Sheet as an inspiration and a guide to pursuing your dream.

Follow your Action Steps as you've scheduled them, and do give yourself room for flexibility. Life is subject to change without notice, and dates have to be adjusted. However, it is crucial that you stick to your Target Date for the completion of your process. Keep that date consciously in mind, together with the mental image you've visualized for your end result.

I can't say it too often: stay focused on your goal, your intention. Don't allow yourself to get bogged down in the difficulty of what you're attempting or the distance yet to go. For example, as a part of my own personal program of physical workouts, I set a goal daily of a hundred sit-ups. I refuse to think, "Oh, gee, I've only done sixty-two and it's getting hard. It's still such a long way to a hundred." In fact, I remind myself to focus on what lies *beyond* the number one hundred, which is on achieving a flat stomach, stronger abdominal muscles, and better all-around health.

> **Follow your dream and watch it unfold.**

Similarly, if your goal is learning to play the guitar, don't despair over your first faltering steps. Don't let yourself be discouraged by the blue notes, the sore fingers, the realization that learning to play well can be a difficult, long-term process. Stay focused on *what you intend to accomplish*—the ability to play that guitar at the level that gives you pleasure and a sense of artistic expression. You'll get there.

Apply my advice to whatever your goal is, whatever your intentions are. Keep looking ahead at the vision you've created. Follow your dream, and watch it unfold!

Conclusion: Transcend Your Workday World

Are you ready to do this? Really do it, not just dream about it and talk about it? Are you ready to plunge into your bright future with confidence and zest, just as a champion diver takes flight from the edge of the diving tower?

Intention + Commitment = Reality

The fact that you are reading this book demonstrates your good intentions—your desire to change your working habits, win back time and energy for those activities that make your life truly worth living, and pursue your dreams.

In these final pages, I want you to focus on a positive fact about intentions. *The power of your intentions, coupled with your commitment to a goal, can—and will—determine your reality.*

This is not wishful thinking; this is a fact. We have seen this fact in action time and again. How could Lance Armstrong have recovered from serious cancer to become one of the greatest athletes of all time, a multiple winner of the Tour de France bicycle race? How was it that Abraham Lincoln and Franklin Delano Roosevelt overcame crushing illnesses to be two of America's most revered presidents? How did the great singer Marian Anderson burst through the racial barrier in 1939 to become hailed as the "voice of the century"? These were people who, through an extraordinary level of commitment, turned their intentions into reality. They each had a remarkable gift, and yet the promise of that gift would never have become a reality unless they *intended* to develop it and *committed* themselves to pursuing their life goals.

Your intentions need not be as ambitious as these examples. However, if you want to achieve your life goals, your level of commitment must be strong. The more arduous or distant your goal—that is, the more *unreasonable* your goal is—the stronger your commitment has to be.

Many sages and prophets have testified to the power of the human will and the ability to connect our desires, through commitment or faith, with a force that seems to come from outside ourselves. In the words of the great mountaineer W. H. Murray:

> Concerning all acts of initiative (and creation), there is one elementary truth, the ignorance of which kills countless ideas and splendid plans: that the moment one definitely commits oneself, then Providence moves, too. All sorts of things occur to help one that would never otherwise have occurred.

—W. H. Murray, writing of the 1951 Scottish Himalaya Expedition

Do you see the point? Success comes not from a divine source that randomly intervenes in human activity, but from *human commitment* so strong that it seems to enlist the forces of the universe in its cause.

That may sound like highblown language. Perhaps you're thinking, all I want to do is learn to bake a perfect soufflé or break ninety on the golf course. For many of us, though, bursting out of our old patterns is daunting. We can get bogged down in inertia and fail to see that our dreams are not "idle dreams," but blueprints for a better life.

Thinking positively is not just a cliché from a vintage book of pop philosophy. It is the key to living our lives with verve and striding into the future with the knowledge that we can make our best intentions real. So take your dreams, your visions, your hopes, and your intentions seriously. Reach deep inside yourself and build there a sense of commitment that will

> **Success comes from human commitment so strong that it seems to enlist the forces of the universe in its cause.**

never be shaken, come what may. Construct a plan that will get you from here to where you want to be. Take action, and stay focused.

For whom are you doing this?

Keep in mind what I said in the Personal Reward section of your Goal Action Sheet. You should be thinking about the benefits *you personally* will gain by achieving your goal. This means that, in this exercise, you are not to focus on the benefits to your company, your family, or anybody other than yourself.

Now I don't mean to say you should be selfish, or that you should try to live hermit-like, removed from family and community. Nor am I saying that you should not pursue a goal that is altruistic, if serving others is your life's calling. My point is that if you truly want to change your life, you need to concentrate on yourself first.

Think, for a moment, about something we hear aboard commercial airliners just before take-off. There's a sentence in the flight attendant's instructions about the use of emergency oxygen masks that goes, "Those of you with small children, please place *your* oxygen mask on first; then attend to your child."

If you are a parent, this instruction runs contrary to your instincts. Why should you take care of your needs before you attend to your child?

Upon examination, the answer is perfectly logical: In the case of a sudden loss of cabin pressure, there is a danger that passengers will lose consciousness. If you were to begin putting your child's oxygen mask on first, you might become unconscious before you can protect your child, and the result could place you both in jeopardy. The rule about helping yourself first is sensible and, in its own way, compassionate; the reason behind it is that you cannot help others unless your own needs are met.

I ask you to apply that principle to building your new life. Even if your life goals are essentially altruistic, your personal needs must be attended to. If you and I are to serve others—our family, our community—we can only do so if we make sure our own needs are met. Thus it is not out of selfishness or egocentrism that we consider our goals in terms of how we ourselves will benefit; it is out of the understanding that whatever kind of life we wish to create, we must be strong, self-caring, and confident in our own right.

Full circle

We have come full circle from the beginning of this book. We've developed techniques that add up to a method of organization and efficiency to manage your workload. The tools in your Instant Productivity Toolkit are not an end in themselves, but a means to something far more important: realizing your life's dreams.

So again I say to you, *Go for it!* Make good use of your newfound freedom. Capture your dreams and envision them. Pursue them with passion—and with a plan. Commit yourself to turning your intentions into reality and watch what happens.

You can do it!

Dear Reader,

In order to better serve you, I'd like you to have templates for the Virtual In-Tray (see page 49), Turtle Sheets (page 68), and the Goal Action Sheet (page 217). Simply send me your email address and I will promptly send you PDF files of these documents, at no cost to you.

Send your request to: toolkit@chaosover.com

Len Merson